Teachers of the Deaf:
Descriptive Profiles

Teachers of the Deaf

Descriptive Profiles

Edward E. Corbett, Jr.
Carl J. Jensema

Gallaudet College Press
Washington, D.C.

Published by the Gallaudet College Press
Kendall Green, Washington, D.C. 20002

Library of Congress Catalog Card Number 80-84605

Gallaudet College is an equal opportunity employer/educational
institution. Programs and services offered by Gallaudet College
receive substantial financial support from the Department of
Education.

ISBN 0-913580-64-3

Of all the areas of special education, there is one that is perhaps a little more special than the rest. This, of course, would be education of the deaf. The first special education program in history originated with Ponce de Leon's work with deaf children in sixteenth-century Spain. The physiological methods used with retarded people and Montessori's sense training techniques are based in the work of early French and Spanish teachers of the deaf.

In the United States, the American School for the Deaf was not only the pioneer in special education but was also the first school of any kind to develop vocational training. Gallaudet College, established during the Civil War, remains the only liberal arts college for the handicapped in the world. The National Technical Institute for the Deaf fulfills the same role in technical education. Today programs for retarded, autistic, and multiply handicapped individuals are drawing on the experience and expertise of teachers of the deaf to develop modifications of American Sign Language to stimulate language and communication development.

It is clear that teachers of the deaf have made contributions far in excess of their numbers not only to their own field, but also to all aspects of special education and to regular education in general. These contributions are interesting given the changes in the composition of the teaching facilities of most programs. During the first part of the nineteenth century, the field apparently was dominated by male teachers trained at elite, exclusive Eastern colleges. Many of the teachers either were trained ministers or had a religious orientation. Deaf teachers of the deaf also played a significant role.

Over a period of more than 100 years there has been a steady change in the characteristics of teachers of the deaf. The rubella epidemic of the early 1960's, the establishment and spread of specialized post-secondary programs, the extension of services to racial and ethnic minorities, and the increase in placement options have led to an unprecedented increase in the numbers of deaf children in educational programs and a concomitant increase in the number of teachers of the deaf.

Teachers of the Deaf: Descriptive Profiles by Edward E. Corbett, Jr. and Carl J. Jensema provides us for the first time with a comprehensive view of the population of teachers of the deaf that has developed over the past two decades to meet new challenges and needs. The authors present a wealth of information related to training, socio-economic status, education, race, sex, hearing status, and job responsibilities. The material not only provides data concerning present circumstances but also will be invaluable for educators and teacher trainers in years to come. For example, we learn that the typical teacher of the deaf is young, female, highly-educated, hearing, and white. The authors point out the discrepancy inherent in the fact that only five percent of the teachers are non-white serving a population in which approximately one hearing-impaired student in three is non-white. The implications for the recruitment and training of non-white teachers of the deaf, as well as for increasing the sensitivity of white teachers, are unmistakable.

Another area highlighted by the data is the role of deaf teachers of the deaf. Typically deaf teachers are under-represented as itinerant and resource room teachers and have not been utilized at the preschool and elementary grade levels. Given their own experience and probably greater sensitivity to the needs of deaf children, educational programs should be moving toward full participation of deaf teachers of the deaf with all age groups in all settings.

It is significant that this book grew out of collaboration between the authors in relationship to Dr. Corbett's doctoral dissertation in Special Education Administration at Gallaudet College. Dr. Corbett is the first individual to receive a Ph.D. from Gallaudet, and Dr. Jensema was chairperson of the dissertation committee. *Teachers of the Deaf: Descriptive*

Profiles represents a major contribution to the field of education of the deaf. It also sets a standard and presents a high level of expectation for work to come.

Donald F. Moores, Ph.D.

Contents

List of Tables

This book is an attempt to describe statistically the characteristics of the population of teachers in special education
programs serving the hearing impaired at the elementary and
secondary levels throughout the United States. Data were
received by mail from 4,887 teachers who were actively
teaching during the 1978-1979 school year in 594 educational
programs across the nation. The information collected focused
on a variety of questions related to the teachers' personal
characteristics, educational background, certification status,
professional organization affiliation, teaching experience,
communication preferences, income, handicapping conditions,
and hearing status. The book provides an overview at the
national level of the labor force participation of a specific
teaching group as compared to a general teaching group
(teachers in public school programs) and represents baseline
data which can be used as a profile for improving the teaching
population and expanding educational opportunities.

Acknowledgements

The long process of bringing this project to completion could not have been accomplished without the assistance of many individuals. The writers would like to express their sincerest gratitude to those persons who generously donated their time, criticism, and encouragement.

Dr. Thomas A. Mayes, Dr. Edmond J. Skinski, Dr. Doin E. Hicks, Dr. Gilbert L. Delgado, and Dr. Michael L. Supley served as members of Dr. Corbett's doctoral committee and gave freely of their time in constructive criticism.

Mr. John T. C. Yeh of Integrated Microcomputer Systems, Inc., and Mr. John K. Woo of the Office of Demographic Studies at Gallaudet College spent many hours developing and testing the computer programs.

Dr. Clarence M. Williams, Dr. Michael A. Karchmer, and Dr. Gilbert L. Delgado helped underwrite the expenses in materials, printing, postage, and the use of computer time.

Many others, although not named, lent a hand with the computer data entry task.

And, finally, Mary Ann and Corinne provided love, criticism, counsel, and pure motivation.

One

Hearing impairment is a widespread disability which affects 13 million people in this country alone. According to *The Deaf Population of the United States* (Schein and Delk, 1974), more people suffer from hearing impairment than any other chronic disability. Of these 13 million people, almost 2 million are "deaf," meaning they cannot hear and understand speech for normal life purposes. Of this deaf population, over 50,000 are known to be 18 years of age or younger, and attend an elementary or secondary school program for the hearing impaired within the United States.

There are many causes of deafness. Many hearing-impaired people do not know the exact cause of their deafness. Heredity is sometimes one of the factors. Still other cases exist which were medically avoidable but occurred despite known methods of prevention. The most outstanding and most recent case of this latter type is the major rubella epidemic which struck this country between 1963 and 1965. This one disease, which was contracted by many pregnant women, caused an estimated

8,000 infants to be born deaf (Desmond, Note 1). This large influx of hearing-impaired children led to a swelling enrollment in elementary, secondary, and now post-secondary programs which school systems are forced to cope with.

When a child is congenitally deaf (born deaf) or when deafness occurs before the acquisition of language (pre-lingual), usually before age three, the greatest handicap is being cut off from the normal means of acquiring and transmitting language. These deaf people have no language frame of reference when learning to speak, write or speechread.

An Historical Overview

Although several references are available regarding the historical development of the education of the hearing impaired in the United States (Bender, 1970; Brill, 1974; and Moores, 1978), few studies describe the characteristics of teachers of the hearing impaired.

Brill (1974) provided an excellent overview of the preparation of these teachers between 1817 and 1970. He found that the early teachers of the hearing impaired (1817-1860) were, for the most part, men who had learned how to teach hearing-impaired children through on-the-job training supplemented by instruction in the language of signs. When the Civil War broke out, many of these male teachers were drafted into serving their country. This caused a severe teacher shortage, which was filled by female teachers, who had less on-the-job training. At the same time, there was a rapid growth in numbers of educational programs serving hearing-impaired children. This increase in programs also gave more women the opportunity to enter the teaching profession. The result was an increase in women teachers of the hearing impaired from 12% in 1857 to 67% in 1894.

According to Brill (1974) the years 1864, 1866, and 1891 were landmark years in the annals of education of the hearing impaired in America. Gallaudet College in Washington,

D.C., was established in 1864 as an institution of higher education for hearing-impaired students, which provided an opportunity for large numbers of well-educated hearing handicapped men to enter the teaching field. However, female hearing-impaired students were not admitted to the college until 1887.

In 1866, the first oral school for hearing-impaired students was established. Schools based on the philosophy of oralism, as opposed to communication through sign language, required teachers to become skilled in the specialized instruction of speech and lipreading. Teacher training then focused on this more specialized kind of preparation. This approach excluded many hearing-impaired teachers from teaching because they did not have the speech and lipreading skills. As a result, there was a considerable drop in the population of hearing-impaired teachers between 1866 and the early 1900's.

In 1891 Congress authorized the establishment of a graduate level program at Gallaudet College to prepare people with normal hearing to teach the deaf. This marked the beginning of a formal teacher preparation program on the collegiate level. Prior to this, the major source of teachers was residential schools for the deaf who had developed their own training programs (Moores, 1978).

The Conference of Executives of American Schools for the Deaf (CEASD) met in the early 1930's to help establish curriculum on education of the hearing impaired for teacher training programs. This curriculum development enabled schools to establish collegiate affiliations resulting in a more standardized program of training teachers.

Brill, himself, was a key figure in developing a study which led to the establishment of a more professional set of standards for preparation and training of these teachers.

In the 1960's the federal government, especially the Bureau of Education for the Handicapped, provided funds and stipends for a number of colleges and universities to develop programs for teacher preparation work in the education of the hearing impaired. Through these financial incentives, a total of 1,196 individuals completed training programs in 1974 from 71 colleges and universities in 32 states and the District of Columbia (Moores, 1978).

The best available estimate of the number of teachers of hearing-impaired children is found in two sources: the *American Annals of the Deaf Reference Issue, 1979* (Craig & Craig, 1979) and an article by Rawlings and Trybus (1978) of the Office of Demographic Studies (ODS) at Gallaudet College, Washington, D.C. Both sources estimate that there are about 10,000 teachers of the hearing impaired in the United States. According to the most recent Rawlings and Trybus study (1978) the student-teacher ratio was 6:1.

The Purpose of this Book

The trained professionals who deal with deaf students on a day-to-day basis are the teachers of the hearing impaired in residential and day school programs around the country. They are as unique and complex as each of their students and surely as important.

In this book we will describe as accurately as possible the teachers of the hearing impaired, the prevailing practices in teaching, and the trends developing in the education of the hearing impaired. The key word is *describe*; this was not an experimental study, but a descriptive one. It was not the objective of this study to eliminate or control all related variables. The study does not outline what the teaching field in education of the hearing impaired should be, but rather examines the present situation to provide baseline data for the future. It is an attempt to profile a number of useful and interesting characteristics of this special teaching population in the United States.

Teachers of the Deaf: Descriptive Profiles presents information essential for determining the condition of the teaching population in the education of the hearing impaired. It answers such questions as:

- Is the typical teacher of the hearing impaired most likely to be male or female, hearing or hearing-impaired like the students they teach?
- Is he or she young, middle-aged, or ready for retirement? Will there be a need to replace large numbers of retiring teachers in the near future to insure qualified instructors for the school-aged hearing-impaired population? And do their salaries vary with years of experience, educational degrees, or certification?
- Is there a need to encourage more ethnic minorities into this teaching field to supply role models for the large percentage of non-white deaf students?
- How proficient are teachers in communicating with their students? What modes of communication do they advocate as most successful?
- What teacher training programs have graduated the largest number of teachers currently working in the profession?

As the major source of information on teachers of the hearing impaired in the United States today, this book can help determine whether or not there is an adequate number of trained, competent teachers with the skills required to help each hearing-impaired child reach his or her full potential. It can be used in educational planning, modifications, and decision-making for those people directly responsible for such tasks whether they are administrators, state and national legislators, Department of Education personnel, or other professionals who must deal with the quality of education for the hearing impaired.

The need for this description is further augmented by the fact that teacher preparation and training, work situations and employment opportunities for teachers, both in general and special education, are all undergoing major changes. The General Accounting Office (1976), in its report to the Congress of the United States, stressed the need for federal thrust in training of teachers in general education to prepare themselves adequately in teaching handicapped children as mandated by Public Law 94-142 (the Education for All Handicapped Children Act). This law has caused considerable shifts in training and preparation needs of teachers.

Methodology

This study concentrated on full- and part-time teachers actively employed in schools or programs for the hearing impaired during the 1978-79 school year. It does not include administrators, teacher aides, or others not directly employed as teachers.

In 1978 there were 1,020 schools and programs serving an estimated 69,000 hearing-impaired children between the ages of four and 21 (Rawlings & Trybus, 1978). The authors eliminated 152 educational programs serving less than four hearing-impaired children.

The study instrument was developed, refined, and targeted to collect data on: personal characteristics, educational background, certification status, affiliations with professional organizations, teaching experience, income, communication preferences, handicapping conditions, and hearing status. The study instrument was pre-tested with 50 teachers of the hearing impaired so that any flaws in the design could be detected and eliminated prior to distribution. During the pre-test, each teacher took approximately 15 minutes to complete the form. When the study instrument was ready, 13,700 copies and cover letters were printed and sent to 868 program administrators (see Appendices A and B).

The study was mailed to program administrators in the last week of September, 1978. A total of 595 program administrators responded, representing 68.4% of the 868 educational programs in the study. Review of non-respondents indicated that most of the non-participants were from small programs. The administrators of the participant programs reported 8,443 active teachers. Each teacher was given a study instrument by the program administrator (see Appendix B).

To encourage accurate reporting, teachers were also given postage-paid and printed return envelopes to mail their completed surveys directly to the Department of Administration at Gallaudet College no later than October 31, 1978. School identification numbers were printed on the envelopes for monitoring purposes. Each teacher's response was kept confidential, and no response was identified with any particular teacher. A total of 4,887 surveys were returned out of 8,443 possible respondents for a 57.9% response rate.

The responses were analyzed by computer, and appropriate statistical tables obtained. The following chapters outline the findings.

Two

Personal Characteristics

This chapter describes the personal characteristics of the teachers of the hearing impaired including age, sex, marital status, number of children, ethnicity, and handicapping conditions.

Age

The age of the teachers ranged from 20 to 77 years, with a mean of 33.6 years and a standard deviation of 10.2 years. Nearly 50% of the sample fell between the ages of 20 and 29. The number of teachers in all age groups steadily declined after age 29 for two possible reasons. There has been a sudden influx of teachers in recent years, and teachers have not been making education of the hearing impaired a permanent profession.

There are many teacher training programs scattered throughout the nation, which have graduated an increasing number of teachers of the hearing impaired. The *American Annals of the Deaf Reference Issues* (formerly *Directory of Programs and Services for the Deaf*), shows the number of graduates of these teacher preparation programs has exceeded 500 students each year since 1970. It is suspected that many teachers began to work with hearing-impaired children and then decided to leave this career after a few years, leading to the drop in the age distribution after age 30.

Sex

Females account for 83% of the sample of teachers of the hearing impaired. There is a definite relationship between the age and sex of teachers of the hearing impaired. The mean age of the males in this study was 36.3 years, while for the females the mean was 33.0 years. More than 50% of the female teachers were under age 30 while less than 28% of the male teachers were under this age. The prevalence of young females in the profession is further emphasized when considered in light of the total sample. Of the 4,887 teachers, 2,050 (42%) were

Table 2.1
Distribution of Age Broken down by Sex

	Male		Female	
Age	N	%	N	%
20-24	33	4.0	585	14.4
25-29	195	23.5	1465	36.1
30-34	248	30.0	688	17.0
35-39	96	11.6	361	8.9
40-44	65	7.8	243	6.0
45-49	61	7.3	231	5.7
50-54	53	6.4	179	4.4
55-59	41	4.9	118	2.9
$\geqslant$60	21	2.5	90	2.2
Not Reported	17	2.0	97	2.3
Totals	830	100.0	4057	100.0

young women under the age of 30. Young male teachers under 30 make up less than 5% of the total sample. Although the number of female teachers exceeds the number of male teachers in all age groups, an examination of the percentile distributions seems to indicate that the male teachers tend to remain in the profession longer than female teachers.

Martial Status

Table 2.2 presents statistics on the current marital status of the teachers. The majority (61%) were married, but, as might be expected in a population which has a large number of relatively young people, a sizable proportion (31%) were single.

Interesting relationships between age, sex, and marital status emerged in the data. The mean age of single teachers was 29.7 years and for married teachers the mean age was 34.8 years. For those who were divorced the mean was 36.8 years. Marital status seems to be important to the continued employment of female teachers. Among those under 30 years of age, the percentage distributions of male and female marital status are about equal. Among teachers over 30 a larger proportion of the males are married (81% versus 66%). Further, the percentage of divorced females is considerably larger than the percentage of divorced males among those over 30. Although there are other ways in which these data may be interpreted, a possible explanation is that female teachers tend to leave the teaching field after marriage but to return to it if the marriage breaks up. Males appear to remain in the profession longer and may be less likely to have their careers terminated by marriage.

Number of Children

Because so many teachers were single, a large majority (62%) had no children. Among those teachers who did have children, two children predominated. The mean age of those teachers who had children was 40.3 years. A larger percentage of the males had children (56% versus 34%), but among those who had children, there was no significant difference in the distribution of children among males and females. For both sexes

Table 2.2
Marital Status

	Single		Married		Widowed		Divorced		Total	
	N	%	N	%	N	%	N	%	N	%
All Males *	192	23.1	609	73.4	2	.2	27	3.3	830	100.0
Males under 30	102	44.7	124	54.4			2	.9	228	100.0
Males over 30	84	14.4	474	81.0	2	.3	25	4.3	585	100.0
All Females *	1327	32.7	2378	58.6	61	1.5	291	7.2	4057	100.0
Females under 30	926	45.2	1051	51.3	1	.0	72	3.5	2050	100.0
Females over 30	380	19.9	1259	65.9	58	3.0	213	11.2	1910	100.0
All Subjects	1519	31.1	2987	61.1	63	1.3	318	6.5	4887	100.0

* Note: Age was not reported by 17 males and 97 females.

the average number of children was about 2.3, a figure relatively close to the national average for the United States.

Ethnicity

The population of teachers of the hearing impaired is overwhelmingly dominated by those who classify their ethnic background as "white." Table 2.3 gives a breakdown of the various ethnic categories reported by the teachers in this study. Nonwhite teachers account for only 5% of the sample, a proportion far below their representation in the general population. This under-representation seems to be general, rather than centered on any single subgroup such as males or females. Non-whites as a group are simply not becoming teachers of the hearing impaired.

The small proportion of non-white teachers is unfortunate. Approximately one hearing-impaired student in three has a nonwhite ethnic background (Schildroth, Note 2). These students need adult models of their own race with whom they can identify, and all students would benefit from a more varied and realistic cultural environment. Clearly, the data suggest an urgent need to recruit more non-white teachers of the hearing impaired.

Handicapping Conditions

With the exception of those teachers who have a hearing loss, the situation in regard to teachers who are handicapped is similar to the lack of non-white teachers. According to the 1977-1978 basic demographic data collected by the Office of Demographic Studies, 28% of the students in schools for the hearing impaired have at least one other educationally significant handicap in addition to deafness. In this study it was found that less than 4% of the teachers have a handicap other than hearing impairment. The prevalence of various handicapping conditions is shown in Table 2.4 which gives a breakdown of the types of handicaps which the teachers reported.

Table 2.3
Distribution of Ethnic Background

Ethnicity	N	% of 4887
White	4583	93.8
Black	159	3.3
Spanish-American	30	.6
Oriental	47	1.0
American Indian	12	.2
Other	9	.2
Not Reported	47	1.0
Totals	4887	100.0

Table 2.4
Handicapping Conditions Reported

Condition	N *	% of 4887
Hearing Loss	663	13.6
Heart Disorder	37	.8
Orthopedically Disabled	37	.8
Severe Visual Loss	34	.7
Cerebral Palsy	15	.3
Epilepsy	11	.2
Other	70	1.4

* Note: Some respondents reported multiple handicaps.

Hearing loss is easily the most prevalent handicap among teachers of the hearing impaired, with almost 14% of the teachers reporting this handicap. There are several possible reasons for this finding. First, hearing-impaired people interested in a teaching career may prefer to work with children having a similar handicap. Second, the teaching opportunities for hearing-impaired people tend to be sharply limited except in schools for the hearing impaired. Finally, many schools make an effort to hire qualified hearing-impaired teachers because they feel that these teachers will make excellent models for the students.

Summary
The data indicates a tendency for teachers of the hearing impaired to be young, white, unmarried females who do not have a handicapping condition. If a teacher does have a handicap, it is almost always hearing impairment. Perhaps there are ways to encourage a more balanced teaching population through changes in current training and employment practices.

Three

Hearing Impairment among Teachers

For most teachers of the hearing impaired, hearing loss influences their personal lives as well as their professional careers. This influence may occur because teachers are themselves hearing-impaired or because they have hearing-impaired relatives or friends. It is difficult to imagine a teacher of the hearing impaired who does not have some contact with the hearing impaired outside a classroom environment.

Those teachers who are hearing-impaired form a special group within their profession of educating hearing-impaired students. Many hearing-handicapped teachers are products of the educational system in which they now teach. Although their numbers are not large (they account for 13.5% of the sample in this study), they often bring to their positions an understanding of hearing impairment which is seldom attained by those with normal hearing. This does not mean that the hearing impaired are necessarily better teachers; teaching is a skill, and being hearing-impaired does not automatically qualify a person to teach the hearing impaired. It could mean that a good teacher who is hearing-impaired may have a greater understanding of the students he or she teaches than a teacher who has normal hearing. This greater sensitivity and awareness of student problems is not easily measurable. It may involve a combination of elements such as developing better communication with students, possessing a greater insight into the psychological and social aspects of coping with hearing impairment, or a host of other factors. All of these factors sum up to a tendency (in the opinion of the authors) for teachers who are hearing-impaired to have a little more sensitivity for what it is to be hearing-impaired.

Since the authors consider hearing impairment, or, more accurately, personal knowledge of hearing impairment, to be important, it has been given careful consideration both in the questionnaire and in the analysis of the data of this study. This chapter will focus in some detail upon the prevalence of hearing impairment among the families of the teachers in this study and upon some of the personal characteristics of the teachers who are hearing-impaired.

The questionnaire asked whether a teacher's spouse, children, siblings, grandparents, or other relatives were hearing impaired. The data from this were analyzed separately for teachers who reported a hearing-impaired relative than for those who did not. Table 3.1 presents a frequency distribution of these data. As expected, the presence of hearing-impaired relatives is reported far more frequently among those teachers who reported being hearing-impaired themselves.

Table 3.1 reveals several interesting findings related to hearing loss. First, it confirms the well-known tendency for hearing-impaired individuals to marry others who are hearing-impaired. Almost 45% of the 663 hearing-impaired respondents have hearing-impaired spouses. However, it must be remembered that only 439 are married and so the actual percentage of hearing-impaired teachers who have a hearing-impaired spouse is about 68%. Even this high percentage is probably low in terms

Table 3.1
Hearing-Impaired Relatives

Relative	Hearing-Impaired Respondents Who Have Hearing-Impaired Relatives		Normal Hearing Respondents Who Have Hearing-Impaired Relatives		Total Respondents Who Have Hearing-Impaired Relatives	
	n	% of 663	n	% of 4224	N	% of 4887
Spouse	297	44.8	80	1.9	377	7.7
Children	68	10.3	123	2.9	191	3.9
Parents	137	20.7	334	7.9	471	9.6
Siblings	162	24.4	178	4.2	340	7.0
Grandparents	73	11.0	315	7.5	388	7.9
Other *	94	14.2	380	9.0	474	9.7

*Note: "Other" consisted mostly of aunts, uncles, and cousins.

of the general population of hearing-impaired people, because highly educated hearing-impaired persons (which the respondents certainly are) are more likely to marry persons with normal hearing.

A second interesting point in Table 3.1 is that nearly 8% of the teachers with normal hearing indicated that at least one of their parents was hearing-impaired. The other categories also indicate a somewhat higher percentage of hearing-impaired relatives than would be expected among the general population of this country. This seems to indicate that many teachers with normal hearing are influenced in their decision to become teachers of the hearing impaired by contact with this disability within their family.

Overall, it was found that 70% of the hearing-impaired respondents and 28% of the normal hearing respondents had at least one hearing-impaired relative. When spouses were excluded, these percentages were reduced to 49% and 27%, respectively. The high percentage of hearing-impaired relatives other than spouses is probably partially attributable to inherited hearing impairment, since up to half of all hearing loss is thought to be related to heredity in some way.

This leads the discussion into the area of age at onset and cause of hearing loss among the teachers in this study who are hearing-impaired. Inherited hearing loss is often unrecognized, and many hearing-impaired people do not know why they are are hearing-impaired. Further, inherited hearing loss does not necessarily manifest itself at birth. It is quite possible for genetically related hearing loss to occur later in life. In this study 36% of the hearing-impaired respondents reported being hearing-impaired from birth, 18% lost their hearing between birth and three years of age, and 18% had no known age of loss. Since severe hearing loss is not likely to go unnoticed after infancy, it seems safe to assume that these "unknowns" were, for the most part, hearing-impaired by age three. This means that approximately 70% of the teachers who were hearing-impaired had a prelingual hearing loss.

The hearing-impaired respondents indicated a wide variety of causes as being responsible for their hearing loss. Table 3.2 gives the frequency with which some specific causes were reported. Note that more than 33% of the respondents did not know the cause of their hearing loss. It is suspected that

Table 3.2
Causes of Hearing Loss among Teachers

Cause	N *	% of 663
Heredity	74	11.2
Meningitis	74	11.2
High Fever	41	6.2
Measles	32	4.8
Infections	31	4.7
Accident	17	2.6
Maternal Rubella	14	2.1
Mumps	14	2.1
Otitis Media	13	2.0
Complications of Pregnancy	6	.9
Trauma at Birth	6	.9
Other	121	18.3
Cause Not Determined	222	33.5

* Note: A few teachers reported more than one cause.

inherited hearing impairment played a role in the hearing loss of many of these teachers who reported that the cause of their loss was unknown.

Most of the teachers who reported a hearing loss also reported that their loss was in the severe or profound range. Table 3.3 provides a breakdown of the hearing loss levels reported by the respondents. Nearly 62% of the hearing-impaired respondents reported a loss of over 70 dB in their better ear. Perhaps partly because of the severity of the hearing loss of many hearing-impaired respondents, only 35% (232 of 663) indicated that they wear a hearing aid.

Another point of interest, especially in view of the severe hearing loss of many teachers, is how well the hearing-impaired teachers in this study could speak and discriminate speech when spoken to. The questionnaire contained three items dealing with self-rating of abilities in this area. The results from

Table 3.3
Hearing Loss Levels

Level	N	% of 663
Normal (Less than 27 dB)	38	5.7
Mild (27-40 dB)	49	7.4
Moderate (41-55 dB)	43	6.5
Moderately Severe (56-70 dB)	63	9.5
Severe (71-90 dB)	134	20.2
Profound (Greater than 90 dB)	275	41.5
Not Reported	61	9.2
Totals	663	100.0

these items are expressed in the frequency distributions given in Table 3.4.

More than 37% of the hearing-impaired respondents reported that they cannot discriminate any speech without a hearing aid, and only about 7% reported "normal" speech discrimination without a hearing aid. With an aid the distribution becomes bimodal, with 20% listing their discrimination as "good" and 26% indicating no discrimination. In other words, without a hearing aid a majority of the teachers who are hearing-impaired have very poor speech discrimination. A hearing aid helps some, but many still have little or no speech discrimination. In contrast, almost 64% of the hearing-impaired respondents reported that they have "good" or "normal" speech. The discrepancy between speech discrimination and speech intelligibility raises questions about the validity of the self-rating system used here. It is suspected that the hearing-impaired respondents sometimes overestimated their speech intelligibility.

Table 3.4
Speech and Speech Discrimination among Teachers Who Are Hearing-Impaired

Self-Rating	Discrimination of Normal Conversation				Speech Intelligibility in Speaking to a Stranger	
	Without Aid		With Aid			
	n	% of 663	n	% of 663	N	% of 663
Normal	48	7.2	60	9.0	237	35.7
Good	96	14.5	136	20.5	186	28.1
Fair	105	15.8	65	9.8	107	16.1
Poor	87	13.1	51	7.7	62	9.4
Cannot Discriminate or Not Intelligible	247	37.3	171	25.8	2	.3
No Response	80	12.1	180	27.1	69	10.4
Totals	663	100.0	663	100.0	663	100.0

Communication Skills

There is no topic within the field of hearing impairment that is more controversial or more widely discussed than communication. For example, in the process of doing background work for a monograph (Jensema and Trybus, 1978) on communication methods used with hearing-impaired students, Corbett and Jensema (1978) found more than 400 articles on the topic.

One of the main points of the Jensema and Trybus monograph was that teachers of the hearing impaired and their students seldom relied on a single method of communication. Most teachers and students used some combination of methods. The communication section of the questionnaire used in this study was based on this point and also on the belief that the composition of the combination would be partially related to the level of skill possessed in each communication mode. The questionnaire asked the respondents how frequently they used each of several communication modes and also asked them to rate how skilled they thought they were in each major mode.

Frequency of communication mode usage was rated in four

categories according to the estimated percentage of time used: Always (76-100%), Usually (51-75%), Sometimes (26-50%), and Seldom (0-25%). The communication modes rated were speech, manual signs and fingerspelling, fingerspelling only, gestures, writing, cued speech, and "other." The "other" category was checked by less than 8% of the teachers and represented a variety of methods which usually related to the specific categories listed. The most frequently reported "other" modes were "total communication," "lipreading," "speech-reading," "pantomime," "drawing," "illustrating," "listening," and "auditory training." Table 4.1 gives the frequency with which each communication mode was reportedly used. In this study, as in the study by Jensema and Trybus (1978), teachers clearly indicate that speech and signs with fingerspelling are the most frequently used communication modes. Perhaps the overall results of Table 4.1 are clearer if the four response categories are coded from 1 (seldom) to 4 (always) and the mean value of each communication mode is computed. Since only a few teachers (5.5%) did not mark a speech category while most (92.0%) did not mark an "other" category, it is reasonable to assume that "not recorded" usually implies that a mode is not used. Under this assumption, the "not recorded" cases were coded as 0. The resulting means were calculated and are given at the bottom of Table 4.1.

The data summarized in Table 4.1 were analyzed in terms of the various combinations of communication modes used by the teacher. The results closely parallel the findings of Jensema and Trybus (1978) and will not be reported in detailed tabular form. Essentially, the majority of the respondents were found to base their classroom communication on speech and signs, supplemented by other communication modes. Because an earlier study by Jensema and Trybus (1978) found speech and signs were the basis of classroom communication in educational programs for the hearing impaired, this questionnaire

Table 4.1
Reported Frequency of Communication Mode

Code Value	Frequency of Use	Speech		Signs and Finger-spelling		Finger-spelling Only		Gestures		Writing		Cued Speech		Other	
		N	%	N	%	N	%	N	%	N	%	N	%	N	%
1	Seldom (0-25% of the time)	161	3.3	588	12.0	1955	40.0	1140	23.3	1040	21.3	2332	47.7	96	2.0
2	Sometimes (26-50% of the time)	212	4.3	336	6.9	637	13.0	1513	31.0	1402	28.7	136	2.8	101	2.1
3	Usually (51-75% of the time)	456	9.3	505	10.3	168	3.4	634	13.0	1045	21.4	73	1.5	81	1.7
4	Always (76-100% of the time)	3787	77.5	2851	58.3	87	1.8	383	7.8	365	7.5	42	.9	112	2.3
0	Not Recorded	271	5.5	607	12.4	2040	41.7	1217	24.9	1035	21.2	2305	47.2	4497	92.0
	Totals	4887	100.0	4887	100.0	4887	100.0	4887	100.0	4887	100.0	4887	100.0	4887	100.0
	Mean Usage	3.5		2.9		.8		1.6		1.7		.6		.2	

was designed to access both frequency of communication usage and self-rated skill in speechreading, signs, and finger-spelling. The objective was to examine the relationship between usage and skill, with the belief that those teachers who were skilled in the use of a communication mode were more likely to use it.

For speechreading, signs, and fingerspelling the teachers were asked to rate both their expressive and receptive skills. In the case of speechreading this was defined as "how well people speechread you" and "how well you speechread." Each of the six ratings had the same five-category scale consisting of "very good," "good," "fair," "poor," and "cannot speechread" (or sign or fingerspell, as the case may be). The percentile distribution of these self-rated communication skills is given in Table 4.2. The rating categories were given code values from 4 to 0, with "cannot do" and "not reported" coded as 0. The mean code value for each category was computed and is given at the bottom of Table 4.2. An interesting feature of this table is that for all three modes (speechreading, signs, and finger-spelling) the teachers tended to rate their expressive skills as better than their receptive skills.

The correlations between reported communication mode usage and self-rated communication skill are given in Table 4.3. The use of speech correlates positively (.24) with the teacher's own speechreading skill but had no correlation with the ability of others to speechread the teacher. Further, speech use was negatively correlated with signs and fingerspelling skills. The general impression from the correlations between speech use and communication skill was that a teacher who rated his or her own speechreading skill highly would tend to use more speech, but when sign and fingerspelling skills were rated highly, less speech was used.

A similar pattern is also apparent in the correlations between sign and fingerspelling use and communication skill.

Table 4.2
Communication Skills as Rated by Teachers

Code Value	Skill Category	Speechreading				Sign				Fingerspelling			
		By Others	%	Own Skills	%	Expressive	%	Receptive	%	Expressive	%	Receptive	%
4	Very Good	1235	25.3	535	10.9	1169	23.9	760	15.6	1089	22.3	570	11.7
3	Good	2533	51.8	1272	26.0	1970	40.3	1469	30.1	1980	40.5	1142	23.4
2	Fair	782	16.0	1707	34.9	958	19.6	1519	31.1	1117	22.9	1736	37.5
1	Poor	102	2.1	880	18.0	326	6.7	605	12.4	326	6.8	927	19.0
0	Cannot Do	27	.6	266	5.4	362	7.4	336	6.8	254	5.2	295	6.0
0	Not Reported	208	4.3	228	4.7	102	2.1	198	4.1	121	2.5	217	4.9
	Totals	4887	100.0	4887	100.0	4887	100.0	4887	100.0	4887	100.0	4887	100.0
	Mean Skill	2.9		2.1		2.6		2.3		2.6		2.1	

Table 4.3
Correlations between Communication Usage and
Communication Skill

| | Skills Rated | | | | | |
| | Speechreading | | Signs | | Fingerspelling | |
Skills Used	By Others	Own Skill	Expressive	Receptive	Expressive	Receptive
Speech	−.01	.24	−.18	−.23	−.16	−.24
Signs and Fingerspelling	−.02	−.18	.63	.56	.45	.40
Fingerspelling Only	.07	−.10	.17	.22	.22	.28
Gestures	.07	−.03	.15	.16	.15	.16
Writing	.08	−.03	.12	.14	.16	.17
Cued Speech	.02	.01	−.10	−.08	−.07	−.04

Those skilled in signs and fingerspelling used these modes more frequently, but those skilled in speechreading used signs and fingerspelling less.

An interesting feature of Table 4.3 is that the teachers' rating of how well other people could speechread them had little relationship to how frequently any mode of communication was used. It had been expected that teachers who felt that others could speechread them well would use more speech and less of the other communication modes. Apparently this is not the case. The communication modes used by teachers had little connection with how well others could speechread them.

A word of caution is in order concerning the communication data in this study and the correlations in Table 4.3 in particular. The communication data are based on self-evaluation of both use and skill. Many factors influenced these evaluations, including the communication policies of the schools in which the teachers are employed. The self-evaluations may or may not be accurate and are not necessarily the way others would evaluate the respondents or the way the respondents would be rated on an objective measuring instrument. Further, correlations are linear measures of the relationship between variables, and in this study they are based on imprecise scales having a limited range of variance. This limited range is particularly important because it automatically truncates the size of the correlations which can be obtained. Related to this is the skewness of some of the distributions. The more skewed a distribution is, the more the size of the correlation is likely to be affected. Hence, the communication data discussed in this chapter must be taken as suggestive rather than a truly accurate and objective measurement of the situation.

To examine communication usage and skill in terms of the sex and hearing status of the respondents, the mean ranks for males, females, hearing impaired, and non-hearing impaired were calculated in the same manner as for Tables 4.1 and 4.2. These means are presented in Table 4.4. The table also includes the mean ranks for all respondents for comparison purposes. The usage differences between males and females are centered on speech and signs, with males indicating they used less speech and more signs. In communication skill, males rated themselves as more proficient in both the expressive and receptive aspects of signs and fingerspelling, but less skilled than females in their ability to be speechread by others.

The differences between hearing-impaired and normal hearing respondents is even more sharply defined than among males and females. Hearing-impaired respondents reported less use of speech and greater use of signs and fingerspelling, fingerspelling only, gestures, and writing. As compared to their hearing counterparts, the hearing-impaired respondents gave

Table 4.4
Mean Communication Usage and Skill Ratings According to Sex and Hearing Status

	Sex		Hearing Status		
	Males (n=830)	Females (n=4057)	Hearing Impaired (n=663)	Not Hearing Impaired (n=4334)	All Respondents (N=4887)
Communication Usage:					
Speech	3.0	3.6	2.7	3.6	3.5
Signs and Fingerspelling	3.3	2.8	3.6	2.8	2.9
Fingerspelling Only	.9	.8	1.2	.8	.8
Gestures	1.5	1.6	1.8	1.5	1.6
Writing	1.6	1.8	2.0	1.7	1.7
Cued Speech	.6	.6	.6	.6	.6
Other	.2	.2	.2	.2	.2
Communication Skill:					
Speechreading					
By Others	2.7	3.0	2.7	2.9	2.9
Own Skill	2.2	2.1	2.8	2.0	2.1
Signs					
Expressive	3.0	2.5	3.4	2.5	2.6
Receptive	2.8	2.2	3.3	2.1	2.3
Fingerspelling					
Expressive	3.0	2.6	3.3	2.5	2.6
Receptive	2.6	2.0	3.1	1.9	2.1

higher ratings to their own speechreading skill and in their expressive and receptive sign and fingerspelling skills. However, the hearing-impaired respondents rated themselves lower in the ability of others to speechread them. In other words, the teachers who were hearing-impaired used less speech and apparently placed greater dependence on other communication modes. While they rated themselves high on their own skills in signs, fingerspelling, and speechreading, they indicated some difficulty in making themselves understood to others through speechreading.

Five

Education

In this chapter we will outline the educational preparation of teachers of the hearing impaired, to pinpoint some facts which influence the quality of this professional preparation. The discussion will focus on the general levels of educational attainment, the colleges and universities where the education was pursued, the courses of study taken, and the financing of this education.

Educational Attainment

The best way to provide an overview of the educational level of the teachers in this sample is to present a breakdown of the academic degrees reported. This breakdown is presented in Table 5.1. Over 97% of the sample reported that they had earned a bachelor's degree and 82% had done some additional coursework beyond this. Almost 75% of the teachers said they held a master's degree and 16% had done some additional work beyond the master's. While most teachers continued their for-

Table 5.1
Reported Educational Attainment

Level	N	% of 4887
B.A.	4750	97.2
B.A.+	4011	82.1
M.A.	3657	74.8
M.A.+	800	16.4
Second Master's	87	1.8
Doctorate	17	.3

mal education at least until they had their master's degree, few of those who remained employed as teachers held a doctorate. Either few teachers are completing their doctorate, or those who do complete the requirements for this degree move on to educational administration, college teaching, or other fields of employment.

The educational attainment level was high among all the various subgroups of teachers. No significant differences in educational level were found between ethnic groups or between hearing and hearing-impaired teachers. However, some interesting differences were observed according to the age and sex of the teachers. The mean age of those who had bachelor's degrees was 33.3 years while those few who did not have a bachelor's degree had a mean age of 43.0 years. Apparently those who do not have a bachelor's degree are mostly older teachers who entered the profession before higher academic standards were set. For those who had a master's degree the mean age was 34.6 years, as compared with 32.1 years for those who did not hold a master's degree. Males tended to have a higher level of educational attainment. Almost 92% of the males had taken coursework beyond a bachelor's degree, while only

80% of the females had done so. Among the males, 87% held a master's degree, as compared to 72% of the females.

Undergraduate and Graduate Colleges and Universities

Teachers reported attending hundreds of specific higher education facilities. Of these facilities, only 76 are known to provide teacher preparation programs in the specific area of education of the hearing impaired. A complete list of the names of these 76 teacher preparation programs is given in Appendix D. A summary of the most frequently reported programs is given in Table 5.2 (undergraduate) and Table 5.3 (graduate) according to rank by attendance of the teachers in the study.

Gallaudet College is the most frequently reported educational institute at both the undergraduate and graduate levels of training. This is due primarily to the teachers in this study who are hearing-impaired. Of the 388 teachers who attended Gallaudet as undergraduates, 373 (96%) were hearing-impaired. Of the 210 who did graduate work at Gallaudet, 60 (29%) were hearing-impaired. This is a direct result of the unique nature of Gallaudet College. Except for a few exchange students, all persons enrolled in an undergraduate degree program at Gallaudet are hearing-impaired. The graduate program at Gallaudet is also open to students with normal hearing, but it attracts many hearing-impaired persons who wish to earn a graduate degree.

At the graduate level, Gallaudet is not the only institution which trains a large number of teachers who are hearing-impaired. Of the 552 teachers in this study who reported having a hearing impairment and who had done some graduate work, 95 (17%) attended Western Maryland College (WMC), and 87 (16%) attended California State University at Northridge (CSUN). Together, WMC, CSUN, and Gallaudet account for the graduate level training of more than 40% of the teachers who were hearing-impaired.

Table 5.2
Leading Undergraduate Colleges and Universities Attended

College/University	N *	% of 4887
Gallaudet College	388	7.9
Illinois State University	121	2.5
Eastern Michigan University	109	2.2
University of Northern Colorado	93	2.0
University of Tennessee	88	1.8
Kent State University	79	1.6
University of Wisconsin	73	1.5
Pennsylvania State University	72	1.5
University of Texas	61	1.2
Ball State University	60	1.0
Michigan State University	51	1.0
Augustana College	51	1.0
Trenton State College	50	1.0
All Others	4214	86.2
Not Reported	154	3.2

* Note: Some respondents checked more than one college or university attended.

In contrast, the teachers who did not report a hearing loss displayed no such tendency to attend certain colleges and universities. At the undergraduate level the most frequently mentioned institution (Illinois State University) was reported by only 115 (3%) of the 4,224 hearing teachers. At the graduate level, Gallaudet led with 150 (4%) of the 3,456 hearing teachers who had done graduate work.

Table 5.3
Leading Graduate Colleges and Universities Attended

College/University	N *	% of 4887
Gallaudet College	210	4.3
Western Maryland College	189	3.9
California State University at Northridge	160	3.3
Smith College	119	2.4
University of Tennessee	119	2.4
Teachers College, Columbia University	103	2.1
New York University, Graduate School of Education	101	2.1
California State University at Los Angeles	88	1.8
Canisius College	72	1.5
Hunter College	72	1.5
Ball State University	68	1.4
Lewis and Clark College	66	1.4
University of Pittsburgh	66	1.4
San Francisco State University	64	1.3
University of Kansas	63	1.3
Eastern Michigan University	60	1.2
Georgia State University	59	1.2
Texas Woman's University	59	1.2
University of Arizona	58	1.2
Boston University	51	1.0
Oregon College of Education	50	1.0
Pennsylvania State University	48	1.0
All Others	2650	54.2
Not Recorded	1145	23.4

* Note: Some respondents checked more than one college or university attended.

Major Courses of Study

The teachers in this study varied not only in *where* they studied but also in *what* they studied, especially at the undergraduate level where nearly 100 different majors were reported. In order to put this information in a more manageable form, many of the infrequently reported specific majors were coded into generic categories. For example, biology, geology, engineering, physics, and similar majors were grouped under the heading of "physical sciences." Majors which were reported relatively often, such as elementary education and psychology, were retained under the name reported by the respondents. The frequency distributions which resulted are given in Tables 5.4 and 5.5 for undergraduate and graduate majors, respectively.

At both the undergraduate and graduate level, education of the hearing impaired was the most frequently reported major, but the actual percentage of the sample reporting this major (25% undergraduate and 31% graduate) is not as high as might be expected when the nature of the teacher's employment is considered. However, Tables 5.4 and 5.5 do not indicate the true extent of the specialized training which the teachers may have had in education of the hearing impaired. For example, a teacher who majored in special education with emphasis on education of the hearing impaired may have as many courses related to hearing impairment as a teacher who attended another college and majored in education of the hearing impaired. The point is that majoring in an area other than education of the hearing impaired does not mean that a teacher is inadequately prepared to teach hearing-impaired students. Perhaps a better criterion of adequate training is certification by the Council on Education of the Deaf (CED). This certification and its relation to major courses of study will be discussed in more detail in a later chapter.

Financial Assistance

Over the years the federal government has contributed a great

Table 5.4
Leading Undergraduate Majors Recorded by Teachers

Major	N*	% of 4887
Education of the Hearing Impaired	1204	25.0
Speech Sciences	777	15.9
Elementary Education	718	14.7
English	309	6.3
Education	278	5.7
Special Education	221	4.5
Psychology	205	4.2
Physical Sciences	165	3.4
Audiology	151	3.0
History	149	3.0
Physical Education	146	3.0
Sociology	125	2.6
Home Economics	113	2.3
Art	76	1.6
All Other Majors	727	14.9
Not Recorded	246	5.0

* Note: 3941 reported one undergraduate major; 680 reported two undergraduate majors; 20 reported three undergraduate majors; and, 246 reported no undergraduate major.

deal of financial assistance in various forms to persons preparing to become teachers of the hearing impaired. In this study 2,548 (52%) of the 4,887 teachers reported receiving some form of financial assistance during their training to be teachers of the hearing impaired. Table 5.6 gives a breakdown of the most frequently reported sources of financial assistance.

Table 5.5
Leading Graduate Majors Recorded by Teachers

Major	N*	% of 4887
Education of the Hearing Impaired	1494	30.6
Special Education	502	10.3
Speech Sciences	216	4.4
Education	136	2.8
Audiology	113	2.3
Administration and Supervision	88	1.8
Elementary Education	64	1.3
Counseling	51	1.0
All Other Majors	506	10.4

* Note: 2795 reported one graduate major; 180 reported two graduate majors; 5 reported three graduate majors; and, 2092 reported no major area of graduate study.

Table 5.6
Sources of Financial Assistance

Kind of Assistance	N*	% of 2548**	% of 4887
Scholarships	1165	45.7	23.8
Loan	525	20.6	10.7
Vocational Rehabilitation	171	6.7	3.5
Stipend	144	5.7	2.9
Grant-in-Aid	143	5.6	2.9
Work-Study	117	4.6	2.4

* Note: Some respondents received multiple financial assistance.
** Note: 2548 teachers reported receiving financial assistance.

Scholarship support was the most common form of financial aid, being reported by 24% of the total sample. These scholarships represent a wide variety of awards from many different private individuals and groups as well as from federal, state, and local governments. The category includes not only scholarships, but also fellowships and scholarly grants from foundations. The second most frequently reported source of financial assistance was government and personal loans toward tuition payments and maintenance expenses. These were reported by 11% of the sample. A majority of the loans seem to originate from the National Direct Student Loan program under the National Direct Education Act of 1972.

Financial assistance from state vocational rehabilitation agencies was reported by 171 teachers. Of these, 154 reported that they currently had a handicap. This means that less than 20% of the handicapped teachers in the study reported receiving financial aid from this traditional source. Table 5.7 gives a breakdown of the most common sources of financial aid reported by those teachers who also reported a handicap. Of

Table 5.7
Sources of Financial Assistance for Handicapped Teachers

Kind of Assistance	N*	% of 388**	% of 800**
Scholarship	208	53.6	26.0
Loan	43	11.1	5.4
Vocational Rehabilitation	154	39.7	19.2
Stipend	15	3.9	1.9
Grant-in-Aid	16	4.1	2.0
Work-Study	10	2.6	1.2

* Note: Some respondents received multiple financial assistance.
** Note: 800 teachers reported a handicap and 388 of these reported receiving financial assistance.

the 800 handicapped teachers in this study, 388 (48.5%) reported receiving some form of financial aid. By comparing Table 5.7 with Table 5.6 it can be seen that handicapped teachers receive more aid from vocational rehabilitation and scholarships than their non-handicapped peers and less aid from other sources.

Year College Credits Were Last Earned
Like many other fields, teaching is a profession based on a vast and constantly changing body of knowledge and philosophy. A teacher's awareness and understanding of this information is a very important aspect of his or her effectiveness as a teacher. This has been recognized by schools, government, and professional organizations as well as by individual teachers.

Schools often base their salary schedules on the amount of formal education acquired, and teacher certification by both governmental and professional organizations usually depends on meeting certain course requirements. Whether the motive is to qualify for a higher salary or a particular certificate or simply to become a more knowledgeable educator, for most teachers formal education is an on-going process long after they have gained employment in their chosen field.

The results of the analysis of the data in this study indicated that teachers of the hearing impaired are very actively involved in continuing their education. Table 5.8 shows a breakdown of the most recent year in which the respondents earned college or university credits. More than 36% of the teachers reported earning credits in the year previous to this study and 80% had earned credits within the past five years.

To emphasize the tendency of teachers to continue their formal education after they have begun their teaching careers, a comparison was made of the number of years they taught and the year in which they last earned college or university credit. Among those who taught 10 years or less, 82% had earned

Table 5.8
Year College Credits Last Earned

Year	N	% of 4887
1978	1798	36.8
1977	897	18.4
1976	641	13.1
1975	353	7.2
1974	227	4.6
1973	132	2.7
1972	109	2.2
1971	69	1.4
1970	64	1.3
1965-1969	136	2.8
1960-1964	65	1.3
$\leq$1959	42	.9
Not Reported	355	7.3
Totals	4887	100.0

credit *after* they began teaching. For these teachers, meeting minimum teaching requirements and beginning their teaching career clearly did not signify the end of formal training.

One reason teachers continue their formal education is to meet CED and state course requirements for certification. In the following chapter the general topic of certification of teachers of the hearing impaired will be reviewed, and the data in this study will be examined in light of the respondents' reported certification status.

Certification

In part, the professional preparation and training of teachers of the hearing impaired can be assessed by the number and types of certificates teachers hold. This chapter addresses the topic under two general headings: certification by the Council on Education of the Deaf (CED) and certification by individual states. The difference between these two classifications is, as Brill (1974) has pointed out, that CED certification represents professional recognition of qualifications for teaching while state certification represents a legal requirement for teaching. The CED certificate is granted by a professional body and the state certificate is granted by a political body. Since this distinction is so important, this chapter will treat each type of certification separately.

CED Certification
The professional certification program for teachers of the hearing impaired dates back to 1930 when the Conference of Executives of American Schools for the Deaf (CEASD) decided to develop and publish a set of minimum standards for pre-

paring teachers to work in this profession (Hall, 1931; Long, 1931). This occurred because most preparation programs were school-centered inservice activities. To enhance professional preparation, teaching certificates recognizing teachers for completing the recommended minimum program of professional preparation were needed (CED, 1972). This certification process resulted in more than 6,000 teachers applying for and being granted teaching certificates.

At that time there were three major organizations involved with the education of the hearing impaired—the CEASD, the Alexander Graham Bell Association for the Deaf, and the Convention of American Instructors of the Deaf. These three organizations were urged to meet jointly and form a single professional organization dealing with the teacher certification process for educators of the hearing impaired. The activity brought about the formation of the Council on Education of the Deaf (CED, 1972) whose main accomplishment was the formation and implementation of professional standards for certification as teachers of the hearing impaired.

The CED has become a representative of most persons involved in teaching hearing-impaired children and in the administration of teacher training programs. The CED, in 1972, presented a two-level program of minimum standards as requirements for the certification of instructional personnel. The provisional certification became the initial level for recognizing a teacher's credentials, and the professional certification the highest level.

"Certification by CED" implies that a teacher has met either one of the two-level programs (provisional or professional) of minimum standards for instruction in an educational program serving hearing-impaired children. These standards include the practical and workable requirements considered by the teaching profession as essential for preparation to teach in the field. Thus, a CED certified teacher is expected to have:

(1) a broad general knowledge of the field, (2) the abilities needed to teach in at least one area of specialization, and (3) at least a baccalaureate degree (CED, 1972).

The CED (1972) presented a more comprehensive set of certification requirements with the following definitions encompassing the six areas of professional specialization within a certificate:

Preprimary: identifies teachers who work with children below the age of six. There are two subgroups within this area of specialization and these are as follows:

Infants: identifies teachers who work with parents and hearing-impaired infants in a variety of educational settings.

Nursery: identifies teachers who work with children between the ages of three and six years in a school setting.

Elementary: identifies teachers who work with children across broad curriculum areas from the beginning of formal academic work at approximately the age of six to entrance into a secondary program.

Secondary (academic area): identifies teachers who teach academic subjects to children beyond the elementary grades (e.g., mathematics, social studies, English, science).

Secondary (special subject area): identifies teachers who teach special subjects other than academic subjects to children beyond the elementary grades (e.g., printing, industrial arts, business education, home economics).

Multihandicapped: identifies teachers who teach hearing-handicapped children with additional physical, mental, or emotional handicaps which significantly interfere with educational progress.

Special content area: identifies a teaching professional or resource teacher who works with hearing-impaired children in special curriculum areas that may cross all age levels (e.g., library science, art, speech, media, physical education).

Of the 4,887 teachers in this study, 2,307 (48%) reported that they were certified by the CED. A breakdown of CED certification status indicates that 35% had provisional certificates and 62% had professional certificates.

The specific competency areas of CED certification reported by the sample are given in Table 6.1. Most of the teachers were certified in the elementary (58%) and secondary-academic (26%) categories. The other specialty areas were much less frequently reported. The data seem to indicate a strong tendency for teachers to receive their preparation in the traditional elementary and secondary academic areas.

However, upon closer examination of the data, some real differences in certification appear in relation to the sex and hearing status of the teachers. Males have a slightly higher rate of CED certification than females (53% versus 48%). It is important to note that more than a third of the males are hearing-impaired. When only hearing males and hearing females are considered, the rate of CED certification is about equal. Hearing-impaired teachers are more likely to hold CED certification than teachers with normal hearing (60% versus 47%). Table 6.2 gives a breakdown of the reported areas of CED certification by sex and hearing status. Males and hearing-impaired teachers have very similar percentile distributions, and both are heavily certified in the secondary academic area. By contrast, females and hearing teachers are most often certified in the elementary area. Other differences in the certification rate of the subgroups are apparent in the preprimary and secondary special subject areas.

The implication is that males and hearing-impaired teachers are most likely to be certified to teach at the secondary level, while females with normal hearing are more likely to be certified at the elementary or preprimary level.

Table 6.1
Distribution of CED Certification Specialties

Specialty Area	N *	% of 2370**	n *	%(n/N)
Preprimary	257	10.8		
Infants			45	17.5
Nursery			145	56.4
Not Recorded			67	26.1
Elementary	1367	57.7		
Multihandicapped	169	7.1		
Secondary (Academic)	628	26.5		
Mathematics			106	16.9
Science			95	15.1
History			66	10.5
Social Studies			136	21.7
English			193	30.7
Other			63	10.0
Secondary (Special Subject)	130	5.5		
Business Science			29	22.3
Home Economics			37	28.5
Industrial Arts			22	16.9
Graphic Arts			23	17.7
Other			23	17.7
Special Content Areas	199	8.4		
Art			17	8.5
Library Science			15	7.5
Media			6	3.0
Speech			69	34.7
Physical Education			61	30.7
Other			37	18.6

* Note: Some respondents checked multiple specialty areas.
** Note: 2370 = number of respondents reporting CED certification.

Table 6.2
Reported Areas of CED Certification by Sex and by Hearing Status

Area of Certification	Males N*	Males % of 443**	Females N*	Females % of 1927**	Hearing Impaired N*	Hearing Impaired % of 395**	Hearing N*	Hearing % of 1975**
Prepri-mary	16	3.6	241	12.5	14	3.5	243	12.3
Elemen-tary	130	29.3	1237	64.2	132	33.4	1235	62.5
Multi-handi-capped	26	5.9	143	7.4	16	4.0	153	7.7
Secondary (Academic)	221	49.9	407	21.1	203	51.4	425	21.5
Secondary (Special Subject)	60	13.5	70	3.6	55	13.9	75	3.8
Special Content	55	12.4	144	7.5	45	11.4	154	7.8

  * Note: Some respondents had more than one area of certification.
** Note: Number of teachers reporting CED certification.

State Certification

There appears to be no single document to which persons interested in teaching exceptional children may turn for complete information on specific state certification require-ments (Abeson & Fleury, 1972). Each state is responsible for setting its own legal requirements for teaching the hearing im-paired. These requirements do not necessarily coincide with those of the CED. Maile (1978) did a study of state certification requirements and their relationship to the certification standards of the CED. He found that the CED standards did not have a significant effect on state certification requirements, but that the CED had a greater influence in bringing about higher standards at the collegiate level for preparation of teachers of the hearing impaired.

A number of studies have urged the establishment of uniform state certification requirements. For example, Gilmore and Argyros (1977) pointed out that special education certification requirements should be made compatible with federal and state regulations and have a broadly based understanding and consensus to ensure a free, appropriate public education for every handicapped child in the country. They suggested that the certification be specific to special education certificates with course requirements, competency requirements and extra preparation, training, experience, or education necessary for specializing in specific disability areas. The specific disability areas they listed included: deaf, hard of hearing, mentally retarded, speech and hearing therapy, multiply handicapped, physically handicapped, learning disabled, emotionally disturbed, and visually impaired.

In spite of studies advocating uniform certification standards, little has been done to change the potpourri of requirements which currently exist. Since state certification requirements vary widely from state to state and encompass a broad spectrum of educational and political policy, the topic is a difficult one to study on a national scale. For instance, some states require that teaching credentials be reviewed every five years for certification; other states mandate that assessment of certification requirements be done every 10 years; and some states grant lifetime teaching certificates after minimum requirements are met. Further, there are a number of states which simply accept CED certification as the legal requirement to teach rather than set up their own certification procedure.

Thus, the data on state certification in this study must be considered only in broad terms and with due consideration to the variation which exists in such certification. The most common general categories of state certification are "Standard," "Advanced," and "Provisional." Table 6.3 gives a breakdown of the data into these categories. State certification was held by 82% of the respondents, far more than the 49% which reported CED certification. This result is to be expected, since state certification is usually a legal requirement while CED certification is usually a voluntary professional option. In Table 6.3 note that only 5% of the teachers held advanced state teaching certificates. One reason for this may be that once teachers meet minimum certification requirements, they have little or no incentive to continue upgrading their state certification status. Advanced or specialized certification levels are not always necessarily connected with higher salaries or better employment opportunities.

Table 6.3
Types of State Teaching Certificates Held

Category	N	% of 4887	n	% of 3998
Certified	3998	82.0		
Standard			2187	54.7
Advanced			215	5.4
Provisional			681	17.0
Other			598	15.0
Not Recorded			317	7.9
Not Certified	784	16.0		
Not Recorded	105	2.0		
Totals	4887	100.0	3998	100.0

The distribution of specialized areas of reported state certification is given in Table 6.4. As expected, the hearing-impaired category was the most frequently reported area of state certification specialization, accounting for 62% of the sample. The next three most frequently reported areas of specialization were the generic areas of special education, speech, and elementary education.

As with CED certification, some differences were observed in state certification according to the sex and hearing status of the respondents. Males were less likely to report state certification than females (74% versus 83%), and teachers who had a hearing impairment had a lower certification rate

Table 6.4
Distribution of Specialization Areas in State Teaching Certification

Specialization Area	N*	% of 3998**
Education of the Hearing Impaired	3012	75.3
Special Education	419	10.5
Speech	378	9.4
Elementary Education	221	5.5
Vocational Education	87	2.2
Secondary Education	75	1.9
Language Related	71	1.8
Science Related	43	1.1
Multiply Handicapped	13	.3
Other	182	4.6
Area Not Reported	282	7.0

* Note: Some respondents checked multiple specialty areas.
** Note: 3998 respondents reported having state certificates.

than those who were not hearing-impaired (74% versus 83%).
Differences were also apparent in the areas of certification.
Males were less likely to be certified than females in education
of the hearing impaired, elementary education, and speech, and
were more likely to be certified in science, secondary education,
and vocational areas. The same differences hold true when
hearing-impaired teachers are compared with those having
normal hearing. Table 6.5 gives a breakdown of the distributions of state certification areas by sex and hearing status.

One additional finding in this study is worth noting. Teachers with CED certification had a mean age of 34.7 years while
those who did not hold CED certification were younger, having
a mean age of 32.2 years. For state certification the opposite
was true. Those holding a state certificate had a mean age of
33.3 years and those without state certification had a mean age
of 34.6 years. The differences are not large but they could be
indicative of a tendency for young teachers to be understand-
ably more concerned with state (legal) certification than with
CED (professional) certification.

Although CED and state certification have been discussed
separately, such certification is far from being mutually exclusive. In this study 41% of the teachers reported holding both
types of certificates. Generally, at least one of the two types
is held. Only 9% of the teachers reported they held neither a
CED certificate nor a state certificate.

Certification is an essential feature in the professional life
of teachers of the hearing impaired. It can provide both legal
and professional recognition of their skills, and it serves as one
indication of their participation in the formal structure which
surrounds their profession.

Table 6.5
Reported Areas of State Certification by Sex and by Hearing Status

Area of Certification	Males n*	Males % of 617**	Females n*	Females % of 3381**	Hearing Impaired n*	Hearing Impaired % of 490**	Hearing n*	Hearing % of 3508**
Education of Hearing Impaired	395	64.0	2617	77.4	274	56.0	2738	78.0
Special Education	73	11.8	346	10.2	57	11.6	362	10.3
Speech	40	6.5	338	10.2	18	3.7	360	10.3
Elementary Education	19	3.1	202	6.0	16	3.3	205	5.8
Vocational	43	7.0	44	1.3	36	7.3	51	1.4
Secondary	29	4.7	46	1.4	27	5.5	48	1.4
Language Related	11	1.8	54	1.6	15	3.1	56	1.6
Science Related	23	3.7	20	.6	23	4.7	20	.9
Multiply Handicapped	1	.1	12	.4	0	.0	13	.4
Other Areas	49	7.9	133	3.9	53	10.8	129	3.7

* Note: Some respondents had more than one area of certification.
** Note: Number of teachers reporting state certification.

Seven

Teaching Experience

All the respondents in this study were actively employed as teachers of the hearing impaired at the time the data were collected. However, their past experience as teachers was not necessarily limited to teaching the hearing impaired. Their experience varied, and in this chapter an attempt will be made to describe the amount and type of this experience and its relationship to certain other variables.

Table 7.1 gives a breakdown of the respondents' number of years of teaching experience in education of the hearing impaired, in other types of special education, in general education, and the total number of years taught in all environments. Although most teachers have concentrated their careers exclusively on education of the hearing impaired, a considerable number also report having taught in other areas of special education (13%) and/or in general education (21%). Among those who taught in areas of special education other than hearing impairment, the mean was 3.0 years and the median was 2.1 years. For those who had taught in general education, the mean and median were 4.4 and 2.7 years, respectively.

Table 7.1
Years of Teaching Experience

Years Taught	All Environments N	%	Education of Hearing Impaired N	%	Other Special Education N	%	General Education N	%
None Reported	291	6.0	401	8.2	4256	87.1	3877	79.3
1	309	6.3	420	8.6	236	4.8	280	5.7
2	461	9.4	523	10.7	135	2.8	202	4.1
3	448	9.2	503	10.3	83	1.7	130	2.7
4	433	8.9	420	8.6	47	1.0	83	1.7
5	389	8.0	408	8.3	38	.8	65	1.3
6	332	6.8	306	6.3	28	.6	43	.9
7	298	6.1	274	5.6	21	.4	36	.7
8	254	5.2	281	5.7	11	.2	29	.6
9	186	3.8	208	4.3	5	.1	13	.3
10	242	5.0	208	4.3	10	.2	29	.6
11-15	537	10.9	474	9.7	14	.3	70	1.4
16-20	325	6.6	227	4.6	2	.0	20	.4
>20	382	7.8	234	4.8	1	.0	10	.2
Totals	4887	100.0	4887	100.0	4887	100.0	4887	100.0

The number of teachers who have taught in areas other than education of the deaf appears higher than might be expected. Remember that this study includes only those respondent teachers who were currently teaching in educational programs for the hearing impaired. Many other teachers trained in education of the hearing impaired may be employed in other teaching environments, and some of these may eventually return to teaching the hearing impaired.

The data seem to suggest that part of the "teacher drop-out" referred to in earlier chapters is actually a movement among types of teaching rather than a movement away from the teaching profession. As teachers continue through their careers many of them tend to branch out and expand their area of experience. For example, among those teachers who were under 30 years of age, only 10% had taught in areas of special education other than hearing impairment and less than 8% had taught in general education. Among teachers 30 years of age or older, 16% had taught in other areas of special education and 32% had taught in general education.

The total number of years taught in all environments varied up to 54 years with a mean of 8.6 years. However, the distribution was very skewed and the median number of years was only 6.3. This, coupled with the fact that about half the teachers were under 30 years old, suggests that although there is movement within areas of teaching, and the number of new teachers graduating from colleges and universities has increased in recent years, many teachers probably do leave the teaching profession permanently soon after beginning their careers.

Mobility is not limited to leaving the profession or moving to another type of teaching. Many teachers remain teachers of the hearing impaired but are employed at a particular school only a few years. Table 7.2 gives a breakdown of the number of years the teachers in this study reported having worked in their present school system at the time the data were collected. Although periods up to 43 years were reported, the mean was only 6.2 years and the median was 4.4. Less than 19% of the teachers had taught in their current school for more than 10 years.

The mean of the total number of years of teaching experience was 8.6 years, and the mean of the number of years in their present school was 6.2. There is a difference of only 2.4 years between these means, a finding which may imply that the average teacher has taught at only one other school during his or her career. The image of a teacher who moves to a new school every year or two seems to have little support. It is suspected that when movement between schools does occur, it is most frequently during the early years of a teacher's career.

Another way of looking at the data is to create a new variable by subtracting the number of years taught at the teacher's present school from the total number of years taught at other schools before joining the staff of the teacher's current school. A breakdown of this new variable is given in Table 7.3. A comparison of Tables 7.2 and 7.3 seems to indicate that a majority of the teachers were currently employed either at the school in which they began their careers or at a school to which they moved within five years of beginning their careers. As

Table 7.2
Number of Years Taught in Present School/Program

Years	N	% of 4887
1-5	2765	56.6
6-10	1213	24.8
11-15	396	8.1
16-20	177	3.6
>20	170	3.5
Not Recorded	166	3.4
Totals	4887	100.0

Table 7.3
Estimated Number of Years Taught before Being Employed at Current School

Years	N	% of 2276*	% of 4887
0 or Missing Data	2611	—	53.4
1-5	1509	66.3	30.9
6-10	465	20.4	9.5
11-15	176	7.7	3.6
16-20	76	3.3	1.6
>20	50	2.2	1.0
Totals	4887	100.0	100.0

* Note: 2276 teachers are estimated to have been employed as teachers before being employed at their current school.

pointed out a number of times, the respondents are relatively young, but even when this is taken into consideration there is evidence that the group maintains stable employment.

A study by Jensema (1977) found evidence which suggested that teachers of the hearing impaired who were themselves hearing impaired were more likely to remain in the profession and also more likely to remain employed at a particular school. The data in this study give some support to this observation. Table 7.4 provides a breakdown of the total number of years of teaching experience reported by the teachers who were hearing impaired, a breakdown of the number of years this group had taught in their present school, and a breakdown of the estimated number of years they taught in other schools. Table 7.4 can be compared with the information in Tables 7.1, 7.2, and 7.3. Teachers who reported they are hearing-impaired tended to have taught longer, both in terms of their career and

Table 7.4
Breakdown of Years Taught by Teachers Who Are Hearing-Impaired

Years	Total Taught		Present School		Other Schools (Estimated)	
	N	%	N	%	N	%
0 or Missing Data	29	4.4	31	4.7	366	55.2
1-5	220	33.2	307	46.3	174	26.2
6-10	181	27.3	166	25.0	67	10.1
11-15	83	12.5	69	10.4	32	4.8
16-20	65	9.8	36	5.4	14	2.1
>20	85	12.8	54	8.1	10	1.5
Totals	663	100.0	663	100.0	663	100.0

in terms of employment at their current school, than teachers who did not report a hearing impairment. They also were more apt to have a somewhat shorter estimated length of employment at other schools before starting at their current place of employment. Additional evidence for the belief that teachers who are hearing-impaired remain in the profession longer may be found by noting that these teachers had an average age of 37.7 years, as compared to 33.5 years for the sample as a whole. The findings of Jensema's 1977 study seem to be supported by the data reported here.

Differences in the distribution of the amount of teaching experience were also found according to the respondents' sex. Because more than one third of the male teachers were hearing-impaired, and because teaching experience seems related to hearing impairment, the 663 hearing-impaired teachers were excluded, and a comparison of hearing males and females was conducted. Table 7.5 gives a breakdown of the years of teaching experience reported by the teachers in this study who did not report having a hearing impairment.

Examination of Table 7.5 indicates that males have more total years of teaching experience and also were employed longer in their present school. However, percentile distribution differences are found only up to about 15 years of experience. Beyond 15 years, there seems to be no essential difference in either distribution. Further, there seems to be little difference between males and females in the number of years taught in schools other than their present one. Interpretation of Table 7.5 is difficult, but perhaps two factors are at work. First, a proportion of the females may be leaving the profession after a few years of teaching, possibly because of marriage and childbearing. This would increase the percentage of female teachers having one to five years experience. Second, the majority of administrators in schools for the hearing impaired are male, and many of these administrators are former teachers who have been promoted. This, coupled with the fact that males do not have their careers interrupted by childbearing, may account for differences in distribution of teaching experience.

Table 7.5
Breakdown of Years Taught by Males and Females with Normal Hearing

Years	Total Taught				Present School				Other Schools (Estimated)			
	Males		Females		Males		Females		Males		Females	
	N	%	N	%	N	%	N	%	N	%	N	%
0 or Missing Data	17	3.2	245	6.6	17	3.2	118	3.2	278	52.4	1967	53.2
1-5	189	35.7	1631	44.2	251	47.4	2207	59.7	172	32.4	1163	31.5
6-10	178	33.6	953	25.8	170	32.1	877	23.7	40	7.5	358	9.7
11-15	69	13.0	385	10.4	54	10.2	273	7.4	24	4.5	120	3.2
16-20	35	6.6	225	6.1	24	4.5	117	3.2	9	1.7	53	1.4
>20	42	7.9	255	6.9	14	2.6	102	2.7	7	1.3	33	.9
Totals	530	100.0	3694	100.0	530	100.0	3694	100.0	530	100.0	3694	100.0

Teaching Position Held

In this chapter we will examine the various aspects of the
current teaching positions held by the teachers in this study.
The questionnaire requested information concerning the teacher's type of position, level taught, the number of teaching days
in the current school year, the average number of students per
class, and extra-curricular activities supervised. Each of these
variables will be discussed separately.

Teaching Position

Table 8.1 gives the distribution of the sample according to type
of teaching position held. The vast majority of respondents in
this study were employed as regular full-time teachers. The next
most frequent category was "Other," which was composed of
a variety of special positions, including specialized teaching
such as library, media, private tutorial, and post-secondary
education.

A few words should also be mentioned about a sampling
bias which exists in the data and the influence of this bias on

Table 8.1
Distribution of Teachers by Teaching Positions

Position	N	% of 4887
Supervising Teacher	202	4.1
Regular Teacher	3611	73.9
Resource Teacher	259	5.3
Itinerant Teacher	358	7.3
Substitute Teacher	14	.3
Other	406	8.3
Not Recorded	37	.8
Totals	4887	100.0

the reported teaching positions. For reasons of economy in data collection, 152 schools and programs having less than four hearing-impaired students were not included in this study. The programs which were eliminated probably employ less than 200 teachers total and represent only a small part of the population of nearly 10,000 teachers. However, many of these teachers may have been in categories other than "Regular." Thus, the special types of teachers may be underrepresented to some extent. Further, substitute teachers are poorly represented, probably because most school administrators distributed questionnaires to the teachers who happened to be working on a particular day.

We examined the data to determine whether differences existed in the positions held according to a teacher's sex. Table 8.2 gives the number and percent of males and females in each teaching position. Males were more likely to be supervising teachers and less likely to be itinerant, resource, or substitute teachers.

Table 8.2
Distribution of Teaching Positions According to Sex *

	Males		Females		Total	
Position	n	%	n	%	N	%
Supervising Teacher	60	29.7	142	70.3	202	100.0
Regular Teacher	620	17.2	2991	82.8	3611	100.0
Resource Teacher	33	12.7	226	87.3	259	100.0
Itinerant Teacher	34	9.5	324	90.5	358	100.0
Substitute Teacher	2	14.3	12	85.7	14	100.0
Other	72	17.7	334	82.3	406	100.0
All Positions	821	16.9	4029	83.1	4850	100.0

* Note: This table does not include 37 teachers who had missing data.

Table 8.3
Distribution of Teaching Positions According to Hearing Status *

	Hearing Impaired		Not Hearing Impaired		Total	
Position	n	%	n	%	N	%
Supervising Teacher	30	14.8	172	85.1	202	100.0
Regular Teacher	541	15.0	3070	85.0	3611	100.0
Resource Teacher	16	6.2	243	93.8	259	100.0
Itinerant Teacher	25	7.0	333	93.0	358	100.0
Substitute Teacher	3	21.4	11	78.6	14	100.0
Other	45	11.1	361	88.9	406	100.0
All Positions	660	13.6	4190	86.4	4850	100.0

* Note: This table does not include 37′ teachers who had missing data.

The type of position a teacher holds is somewhat dependent upon hearing status. Table 8.3 gives a breakdown of the proportion of teachers holding each position according to whether they reported a hearing loss. The main feature of Table 8.3 is that teachers who reported a hearing impairment were less likely than those with normal hearing to be resource or itinerant teachers. This may be related to the fact that Jensema (1977) found that teachers who are hearing-impaired are most likely to be employed in residential schools. Such schools usually have fewer resource or itinerant positions.

Education plays a role in the type of position a teacher holds. Table 8.4 gives a breakdown of the distribution of teachers for each position according to whether or not a master's degree was reported. Almost nine out of every 10 supervising teachers held a master's degree. Substitute and itinerant teachers were the least likely to hold a master's degree.

Table 8.4
Distribution of Teaching Positions According to Whether a Master's Degree Was Reported *

Position	Master's Degree		No Master's Degree		Total	
	n	%	n	%	N	%
Supervising Teacher	177	89.4	21	10.6	198	100.0
Regular Teacher	1988	60.2	1313	39.8	3301	100.0
Resource Teacher	169	67.6	81	32.4	250	100.0
Itinerant Teacher	199	57.8	145	42.2	344	100.0
Substitute Teacher	6	42.9	8	57.1	14	100.0
Other	285	73.6	102	26.4	387	100.0
All Positions	2824	62.8	1670	37.2	4494	100.0

* Note: This table does not include 393 teachers who either did not state their position or who did not report whether they held a master's degree.

In addition to education, the years of experience a teacher had also related to the type of position held. Table 8.5 gives the mean number of years of experience in various educational settings reported by the teachers who held specific positions. Supervising teachers had the highest mean years of experience in all settings except general education, and substitute teachers had the least experience. However, it must be kept in mind that all of the distributions on which these means were based were positively skewed. The bulk of the teachers were at the lower end of the experience scale and the number of teachers tapered off as the years of experience increased. This tends to distort the means. For example, the means would be several years lower if those teachers with 30 or 40 years of experience were excluded.

Table 8.5
Mean Years of Experience According to Teaching Position Held

Position	Total Teaching Exper.	Ed. of Hearing Impaired	Other Special Ed.	General Ed.	Present School
Supervising Teacher	13.3	11.6	4.3	4.3	9.6
Regular Teacher	8.4	7.3	2.9	4.3	6.3
Resource Teacher	8.1	6.2	2.3	4.1	5.0
Itinerant Teacher	7.0	5.8	2.8	3.6	4.5
Substitute Teacher	5.3	4.5	*	*	3.7
Other	9.6	7.9	3.5	5.3	6.1
Grand Mean	8.6	7.4	3.0	4.3	6.2

* Note: Data deleted because of small sample size. There were only 14 substitute teachers in this study and only five of these reported experience outside of teaching the hearing impaired.

Level Taught

Since hearing-impaired students often function several years behind their hearing peers academically, many educational programs serving the hearing impaired are ungraded in nature and teachers often find themselves teaching at more than one academic level. To simplify the task of describing the academic levels taught, the questionnaire in this study only asked the teachers to check whether they taught at the preschool, elementary, middle, or senior high level. Even with this simplification many teachers reported teaching at more than one of these levels. Elementary education was the most frequent response, followed by middle and senior high. The "Other" category consisted mostly of teachers engaged in post-secondary education programs and private tutoring outside of school hours.

A point of interest at the time the questionnaire was developed was the extent to which teaching of the hearing impaired centered around the traditional self-contained classroom. It was expected that self-contained classrooms would be most common at the lower academic levels and that their prevalence would decrease at more advanced levels. This proved to be the case. The percentage of teachers who reported teaching in self-contained classrooms at each level was as follows: Preschool = 62.5%, Elementary = 60.2%, Middle = 39.3%, Senior High = 35.2%, and "Other" = 46.0%. These results are not surprising, since the material taught becomes more specialized as the level advances and requires a more specialized teacher. Overall, 52.7% of the teachers reported teaching in a self-contained classroom.

Various other relationships were also investigated. The educational levels taught did not relate to whether the teacher had a master's degree, CED certification, or state certification. However, the level taught was related to the age, sex, and hearing status of the respondents. The mean age of those who reported teaching at the preschool, elementary, middle, and senior high levels was 32.7, 33.0, 33.2, and 34.6 years, respectively. The mean age of those who reported "Other" levels was 34.6 years. The general trend is for older teachers to teach higher levels. The total number of years of teaching experience also follows this pattern in relating to educational level taught. Unfortunately, this study did not include information on the levels taught by each teacher in the past. It cannot be determined whether the results are due to the higher teacher dropout rate at lower educational levels or a tendency for teachers to transfer to teaching higher levels. It is suspected that the first reason may be the primary one because the study shows that the lower levels are composed primarily of hearing females. Hearing females tend to be younger and have less experience than teachers who are male or hearing-impaired.

The percentage of males rises steadily according to educational level. Only 7% of the preschool teachers are male, as compared to 32% of the senior high school teachers. More than half of the male respondents (453 of 830) reported that they taught at the senior high level while less than a quarter of the female teachers (954 of 4,057) did so.

The pattern which holds for males also holds for those who are hearing-impaired, as can be seen in Table 8.6. This table gives the percentage of teachers who are hearing-impaired at each of the educational levels. At the preschool level only 5% of the teachers reported having a hearing impairment, while at the senior high school level the proportion is 22%. Almost half of all teachers who are hearing-impaired teach at the senior high level. Further, the same overall differences by sex were present among the hearing-impaired respondents as for the sample as a whole. Data on this will not be given in tabular form, but it was found that among the hearing-impaired males only 3.7% reported teaching at the preschool level while 8.3% of the hearing-impaired females taught at this level. At the senior high school level the percentages were 63.0% and 40.8%, respectively.

Table 8.6
Educational Levels Taught According to Hearing Status

Level	Hearing Impaired		Not Hearing Impaired		Total	
	n	%	n	%	N	%
Preschool	44	5.1	826	94.9	870	100.0
Elementary	161	7.5	1997	92.5	2158	100.0
Middle	239	14.6	1398	85.4	1637	100.0
Senior High	309	22.0	1098	78.0	1407	100.0
Other	59	14.0	363	86.0	422	100.0
All Subjects*	663	13.6	4224	86.4	4887	100.0

* Note: Some respondents taught at more than one educational level. This row does not represent column totals.

Although male teachers and those who are hearing-impaired have a similar tendency to teach at the upper academic levels, the reasons for this tendency may be quite different. Males have traditionally taught at the upper levels, while females have been more likely to teach at the preschool or elementary level. In the case of teachers who are hearing-impaired, however, the level taught may not always be a matter of individual choice and training. Many educational programs prefer not to employ hearing-impaired teachers at the preschool and elementary levels because of difficulties in teaching speech and speechreading skills to hearing-impaired children. On the other hand, teachers who are hearing-impaired are sometimes given preference at the middle and senior high levels because many schools feel that these teachers provide needed adult models for the students.

Teaching Days
Educational requirements are determined by each state, and

individual states vary in the number of required teaching days per year. A school year is usually about 180 days. When breaking down the number of days per year which the teachers in this study reported teaching, the "180-184" category is by far the most frequent. Within this category, 1,979 teachers, more than 40% of the entire sample, reported that they taught exactly 180 days and the overall mean number of teaching days was also 180.

The authors originally expected the number of teaching days to vary according to teaching position and level taught. For example, we thought that supervising teachers and those who taught at the preschool level would have more teaching days. The data did not bear this out. No important differences were found.

Number of Students in a Class

A frequency distribution of the teachers according to the average number of students they reported having in their classes is given in Table 8.7. The majority of the teachers (58%) reported between five and eight students in their classrooms, with a mean of 6.7 students. Some teachers reported more than 10 students per class. Closer investigation of these cases indicated that they usually involved physical education classes, vocational education classes, and a few other subject areas which are conducive to a larger enrollment.

As was the case with the number of days taught, class size tends to vary with the type of position held and the level taught. Those respondents who were supervising teachers had the largest reported class size with a mean of 8.6 students. Resource teachers and itinerant teachers had the lowest mean class sizes with 5.0 and 4.0 students, respectively. The remaining types of positions had very close to the overall average of 6.7 students. There was very little difference in class size according to level taught. The mean number of students ranged from 6.5 for elementary to 7.2 for high school.

Table 8.7
Average Number of Students Per Class

Number of Students	N	% of 4887
1	262	5.4
2	146	3.0
3	197	4.0
4	346	7.1
5	615	12.6
6	870	17.8
7	651	13.3
8	688	14.1
9	193	3.9
10	198	4.1
11-15	152	3.1
16-20	44	.9
$\geqq$21	49	1.0
Not Recorded	475	9.7
Totals	4887	100.0

In general, the information on class size seems to reflect the acceptance and implementation of the general educational policy mentioned by Brill, Merrill, and Frisina (1973). This policy advances the principle that classes of hearing-impaired children should contain not less than four children nor more than six children for the preschool and primary years, eight for elementary years, and 10 for secondary programs.

Extra-Curricular Activities Supervised
At many schools for the hearing impaired, extra-curricular

activities play a very important part in the educational and social development of the students. Unfortunately, these activities usually receive very marginal financial support from the schools and are often supervised by people who are not teachers of the hearing impaired, such as dormitory counselors and volunteers from the surrounding community. Perhaps the crux of the issue is that many educational programs cannot afford to compensate a teacher adequately for becoming involved in an extra-curricular activity. When this happens, teacher participation and interest may wane after a year or two. In this section some of the characteristics of those teachers who do participate in extra-curricular activities will be explored.

Table 8.8 gives a frequency count of the number of teachers who reported supervising extra-curricular activities in various categories. Only 37% of the teachers reported supervising one or more activities.

Table 8.8
Extra-Curricular Activities Supervised

Activity	N*	% of 4887
Class Sponsor	343	7.0
Clubs	254	5.2
Coaching	337	6.9
Organizations	275	5.6
Recreation	218	4.5
Religious Activities	33	.7
Other	718	14.7
No Reported Participation	3093	63.3

* Note: Some respondents supervised more than one extra-curricular activity.

Some sex differences exist in teacher participation in extra-curricular activities, but these differences are primarily due to male dominance of coaching. Table 8.9 gives the distribution of supervisors in various activities according to sex. Of the 830 males, 176 (21%) reported being coaches while only 161 (4%) of the 4,057 females reported this. The reason for this is that schools now provide a larger number of organized sports for boys than for girls, and coaches are usually of the same sex as the players. In activities other than coaching, male teachers have a higher proportion of their number involved as class sponsors, in clubs, and with school organizations. Overall, a male is considerably more likely to participate in extra-

Table 8.9
Sex Distribution of Extra-Curricular Activity Supervisors

Activity	Male		Female		Total	
	n*	%	n*	%	N*	%
Class Sponsor	92	26.8	251	73.2	343	100.0
Clubs	58	22.8	196	77.2	254	100.0
Coaching	176	52.2	161	47.8	337	100.0
Organizations	72	26.2	203	73.8	275	100.0
Recreation	36	16.5	182	83.5	218	100.0
Religious Activities	5	15.2	28	84.8	33	100.0
Other	118	16.4	600	83.6	718	100.0
Reported Participation	429	23.9	1365	76.1	1794	100.0
No Reported Participation	401	13.0	2692	87.0	3093	100.0
All Subjects	830	17.0	4057	83.0	4887	100.0

* Note: Some respondents supervised more than one activity.

curricular activities than a female. Almost 52% of the males participated in some activity as compared to about 34% of the females.

Variation in the supervision of extra-curricular activities occurs according to hearing status as well as sex. Table 8.10 gives a breakdown of the hearing status of teachers who participate in these activities. A teacher who was hearing-impaired was generally more likely to report participation. Supervision by a hearing-impaired teacher was highest for school organizations and lowest for recreational activities. One interesting point is that by comparing Table 8.9 with Table 8.10 one can

Table 8.10
Hearing Status of Extra-Curricular Activity Supervisors

Activity	Hearing Impaired		Not Hearing Impaired		Total	
	n*	%	n*	%	N*	%
Class Sponsor	95	27.7	248	72.3	343	100.0
Clubs	60	23.6	194	76.4	254	100.0
Coaching	91	27.0	246	73.0	337	100.0
Organizations	89	32.4	186	67.6	275	100.0
Recreation	25	11.5	193	88.5	218	100.0
Religious Activities	5	15.2	28	84.8	33	100.0
Other	93	13.0	625	87.0	718	100.0
No Reported Participation	312	10.1	2781	89.9	3094	100.0
Reported Participation	351	19.6	1443	80.4	1794	100.0
All Subjects	663	13.6	4224	86.4	4887	100.0

* Note: Some respondents supervised more than one activity.

see that among those few teachers who supervised religious activities, all were either hearing-impaired males or hearing females. For some reason no hearing-impaired female or hearing male reported supervision of religious activities.

Subjects Taught

Previously we explored some of the characteristics of the positions held by teachers of the hearing impaired. Now we will examine the subjects taught by the teachers.

As expected, most teachers reported teaching several subjects. The overall average was 3.9 subjects per teacher. Table 9.1 gives the number of teachers who reported teaching each of the various major subject areas. As expected, language was the most frequently taught subject, reported by 67% of the teachers. Whether language was taught as a formal subject in itself or whether it was taught in conjunction with other subjects is not clear. However, since language acquisition is the most arduous learning task facing hearing-impaired students, it is very likely to be an integral part of almost any class. This fact cannot be overemphasized. When a hearing child enters elementary school the process of language learning is basically one of refining existing skills. A hearing-impaired child, on the other hand, may have little or no preconceived notion of language when he or she begins formal education. Teachers of

Table 9.1
Educational Subjects Being Taught

Subjects	N*	% of 4887
Language	3285	67.2
Reading	2904	59.4
Mathematics	2729	55.8
Communication	2366	48.4
Social Studies	2302	47.1
Science	2015	41.2
Art	939	19.2
History	611	12.5
Physical Education	579	11.8
Prevocational	560	11.5
Elective(s)	553	11.3
Driver's Education	109	2.2

* Note: Many respondents checked two or more educational subjects.

the hearing impaired must instill linguistic concepts and begin communication comprehension before academic learning can commence.

Communication is closely connected with language in many schools. In Table 9.1 this subject is the fourth most frequently taught academic area and was reported by 48% of the teachers. The category of communication is something of a generic subject, one which includes speech and auditory training as well as various forms of sign language and other methods of communication. As in the case of language, communication is a subject which permeates almost all other academic areas. Since the communication used by hearing-impaired students is not the ''natural'' language of most teachers of the hearing impaired, especially those who have normal hearing, and since communication plays such an important role in all academic areas, the questionnaire in this study contained items designed to investigate the teachers' perceptions of their communication skills. Those responses were analyzed in Chapter Four: Communication Skills.

In Table 9.1, reading and mathematics rank second and third, respectively, among the most frequently taught subjects. Social studies and science rank fifth and sixth. Notice that after science, the proportion of teachers who reported teaching the succeeding subject areas drops sharply. This seems to indicate that schools are placing heavy emphasis on the traditional fundamentals of education. One interesting point is that more teachers reported teaching art (19%) than history (12%). The reasons for this are speculative, but perhaps they relate to the fact that art is more visually oriented and less dependent upon language.

Finally, a brief explanation should be given concerning the last three categories in Table 9.1. Driver's education is an elective so commonly offered that it was decided to include it as a specific category on the questionnaire. The prevocational category includes those classes which relate to possible future employment skills, such as machine shop, printing, business, and so on. The elective category includes a wide variety of subjects ranging from sex education to crafts. The distinction between the prevocational and elective category is not always clear. For example, some teachers may have considered typing classes as prevocational while others may have included them in the elective category. One common characteristic all three categories have is that they represent classes which are usually offered only at the upper academic levels.

Some distinct differences were found in the data regarding the subjects taught by males and females. Table 9.2 provides the distribution of male and female teachers in each academic area. Males appear to concentrate on teaching prevocational, elective, and driver's education classes. Further, males reported teaching an average of 2.6 subjects while females reported an average of 4.1. Both findings seem to be in line with the earlier observation that males tend to teach at the higher academic levels. For example, high school teachers usually teach in a more specialized subject area and, as mentioned before, many prevocational, elective, or driver's educa-

Table 9.2
Educational Subjects Taught According to Sex of Respondents

Subjects	Male		Female		Total	
	n*	%	n*	%	N*	%
Language	318	9.7	2967	90.3	3285	100.0
Reading	280	9.6	2624	90.4	2904	100.0
Mathematics	352	12.9	2377	87.1	2729	100.0
Communication	204	8.6	2162	91.4	2366	100.0
Social Studies	272	11.8	2030	88.2	2302	100.0
Science	225	11.2	1790	88.8	2015	100.0
Art	46	4.9	893	95.1	939	100.0
History	91	14.9	520	85.1	611	100.0
Physical Education	85	14.7	494	85.3	579	100.0
Prevocational	165	29.5	395	70.5	560	100.0
Elective(s)	113	20.4	440	79.6	553	100.0
Driver's Education	40	36.7	69	63.3	109	100.0
All Subjects	830	17.0	4057	83.0	4887	100.0

* Note: Many respondents checked two or more educational subjects.

tion classes are offered only at the upper academic levels. The same situation holds true in reverse. For example, less than 5% of the art teachers are male, a finding which may relate to the fact that art is usually a required part of the curriculum at the lower academic levels and is often taught by a regular class-room teacher. High school students generally take art only if they have a particular interest or talent in that area.

The data were also examined to determine if differences existed according to hearing status among the subjects taught. Table 9.3 gives the frequency with which hearing loss was

Table 9.3
Educational Subjects Taught According to Hearing Status

Subject	Hearing Impaired		Not Hearing Impaired		Total	
	n*	%	n*	%	N*	%
Language	294	9.0	2991	91.0	3285	100.0
Reading	265	9.1	2639	90.9	2904	100.0
Mathematics	305	11.2	2424	88.8	2729	100.0
Communication	170	7.2	2196	92.8	2366	100.0
Social Studies	236	10.2	2066	89.7	2302	100.0
Science	187	9.3	1828	90.7	2015	100.0
Art	53	5.6	886	94.4	939	100.0
History	53	8.7	558	91.3	611	100.0
Physical Education	59	10.2	520	89.8	579	100.0
Prevocational	100	17.9	460	82.1	560	100.0
Elective(s)	81	14.6	472	85.4	553	100.0
Driver's Education	12	11.0	97	89.0	109	100.0
All Subjects	663	13.6	4224	86.4	4887	100.0

* Note: Many respondents checked two or more educational subjects.

reported among the teachers in each subject category. The differences are not nearly as clearly defined as they were for males and females. Teachers who are hearing-impaired are more prevalent among those who teach prevocational and elective courses, a fact which coincides with the earlier finding that the hearing impaired tend to teach upper academic levels. Overall, those teachers who reported a hearing impairment also reported teaching in fewer subject areas. The average for the hearing impaired was 2.7 subject areas, as compared with 4.1 for those who were not hearing impaired. This is very close to the averages for males and females, perhaps reflecting that both males and hearing-impaired teachers are more likely to teach at the upper academic levels.

The foregoing paragraphs imply that the courses taught were related to the academic level at which teaching was done. Table 9.4 clarifies this issue by presenting the number and percent of teachers at each level who reported teaching courses in each academic area. The table also gives the average number of academic areas taught for each level. Those who reported teaching at the elementary level teach the largest average number of course areas. A clear change in the types of courses most often taught occurs as the level increases. At the preschool and elementary level teachers most often teach the basic educational skills. In the middle and high school levels there is a strong shift towards prevocational and elective courses. The general trend is, as expected, for the courses taught to become more evenly distributed over a broader range as the academic level increases.

One aspect of Table 9.4 which may seem incongruous to some readers is that a few teachers who reported teaching driver's education also reported teaching at the preschool and elementary levels. Some teachers did report teaching at several levels, and a teacher of driver's education may also be responsible for teaching traffic safety or some other topic at the lower levels.

Table 9.4
Subjects Taught by Level Taught

Subject	Preschool		Elementary		Middle		High School		Other	
	N	%*	N	%*	N	%*	N	%*	N	%*
Language	651	74.8	1745	80.9	1012	61.8	678	48.2	244	57.8
Reading	450	51.7	1654	76.6	920	56.2	557	39.6	187	44.3
Mathematics	449	51.6	1532	71.0	785	47.9	509	36.2	173	41.0
Communication	543	62.4	1395	64.6	664	40.6	378	26.9	208	49.3
Social Studies	331	38.0	1342	62.2	697	42.6	417	29.6	106	25.1
Science	308	35.4	1214	56.2	611	37.3	322	22.9	86	20.4
Art	276	31.7	611	28.3	144	8.8	57	4.0	54	12.8
History	55	6.3	307	14.2	307	18.8	241	17.1	27	6.4
Physical Education	204	23.4	350	16.2	141	8.6	90	6.4	46	10.9
Prevocational	41	4.7	134	6.2	241	14.7	288	20.5	82	19.4
Elective(s)	72	8.3	188	8.7	224	13.7	239	17.0	54	12.8
Driver's Education	8	.9	21	1.0	37	2.3	93	6.6	10	2.4
Number Reporting Teaching at Each Level	870		2158		1637		1407		422	
Mean Number of Subject Areas Taught	3.9		4.9		2.4		2.7		3.0	

* Note: Percentages given are based on the number of respondents who reported teaching at each level. Some teachers reported teaching at more than one level.

The data were also examined to determine whether any connection existed between subjects taught and whether a teacher held a CED or state teaching certificate. The authors initially thought that those who taught certain subjects might have a greater rate of certification. Some differences were observed in the certification of teachers who taught specialized subjects usually associated with the higher academic levels. However, these differences were not large and may be due to random fluctuations in the data.

A more relevant question is whether the teachers are certified in the subject areas in which they teach. This is a difficult question to assess and, unfortunately, cannot be adequately answered from the data in this study for two reasons: first, state certification varies widely and many states simply certify a teacher in special education or education of the hearing impaired without specifying the special courses or subjects in which a teacher is qualified. Second, although CED certification involves six major specialties and a number of sub-specialties, fewer than half the respondents reported holding a CED certificate, and many of these did not indicate their major specialty and/or sub-specialty of certification.

A final examination of the data was made to determine variation in subjects taught relative to salary and educational attainment. As expected, no meaningful pattern was found for these variables.

Ten

One of the problems related to the design of the questionnaire in this study was the authors' underestimation of the salary earned by teachers of the hearing impaired. The item on salaries was written in categorical groupings because it was felt that the teachers would be more willing to respond to a list of salary ranges rather than to specify their exact income. It was expected that most teachers would earn about $12,000 or $13,000 for a nine-month school year. Therefore, the salary item was written to cover $9,000 to $15,000 in $1,000 increments. As can be seen from Table 10.1, this range proved to be too low to include nearly one-third of the sample. More than 30% of the teachers indicated that they received over $15,000 per year in school-related income. Although it is not possible to calculate the mean annual income from the data, an estimate of the median income can be obtained. The median salary should be approximately $13,300. This is only a few hundred dollars more than originally expected.

Table 10.1
School-Related Incomes Earned

Income Range	N	% of 4887
<$9,000	183	3.7
$9,000-9,999	275	5.6
$10,000-10,999	586	12.0
$11,000-11,999	659	13.5
$12,000-12,999	642	13.1
$13,000-13,999	535	10.9
$14,000-14,999	459	9.4
≧$15,000	1489	30.5
Income Not Reported	59	1.2
Totals	4887	100.0

Table 10.1 includes only school-related income. The questionnaire also asked the teachers to indicate their non-school-related income. The reason for this is that some teachers may supplement their income through private tutoring or summer employment outside their regular teaching job. More than 73% of the teachers reported no income other than from their school employment. Of the 22% who did earn outside income, less than 8% earned $1,000 or more per year. Although there may have been some reluctance to report non-school income, it is apparent that "moonlighting" is not a widespread practice. One factor in considering the data is that 61% of the sample were married. Many of those teachers who are married may represent a two-income family. Hence, the reported salary of the teachers is not necessarily the total family income.

A strong relationship existed in the data between the sex

of the teachers and both school-related and non-school-related salary. Table 10.2 gives the proportion of males and females at each salary level. The table makes it clear that males are more likely to have a non-school-related income and that they tend to earn more in both the school and non-school settings. On the

Table 10.2
Income According to Sex

Income	Male n	%	Female n	%	Total N	%
Non-School-Related						
None Reported	489	13.6	3091	86.3	3580	100.0
<1,000	182	19.3	759	80.7	941	100.0
$1,000-1,999	64	39.8	97	60.2	161	100.0
$2,000-2,999	34	42.5	46	57.5	80	100.0
≧$3,000	61	48.5	64	51.2	125	100.0
School-Related						
None Reported	9	15.2	50	84.7	59	100.0
<$9,000	14	7.7	169	92.3	183	100.0
$9,000-9,999	31	11.3	244	88.7	275	100.0
$10,000-10,999	59	10.1	527	89.9	586	100.0
$11,000-11,999	73	11.1	586	88.9	659	100.0
$12,000-12,999	94	14.6	548	85.4	642	100.0
$13,000-13,999	90	16.8	445	83.2	535	100.0
$14,000-14,999	86	18.7	373	81.3	459	100.0
≧$15,000	374	25.1	1115	74.9	1489	100.0
All Subjects	830	17.0	4057	83.0	4887	100.0

other hand, the finding that males have a higher income is probably not indicative of salary discrimination on the basis of sex, since it has been previously shown that the male teachers in this study also tend to have a somewhat higher level of education and experience than females. It will be seen later in this chapter that both education and experience are related to salary.

One of the points of interest at the time this study was developed was whether there was any evidence of salary discrimination on the basis of hearing loss. It was felt that since teachers who are hearing-impaired are limited in their teaching opportunities outside the field of hearing impairment, they may be obligated to accept lower salaries within the field. However, the data give absolutely no evidence of this. In fact, hearing-impaired teachers as a group seemed to command slightly higher salaries, possibly because they remained in the profession somewhat longer than their hearing counterparts, and salary is often related to length of teaching service. Further, although teachers who were hearing-impaired reported non-school-related salaries no more frequently than those who had normal hearing, those who did have outside income reported a higher salary. Among those who reported non-school income of $3,000 or more, 24% were hearing-impaired. The data on the relation between hearing status and income is summarized in Table 10.3.

Although hearing status had little influence on the salary earned by teachers of the hearing impaired, whether or not a teacher held a master's degree was definitely an important factor in school-related income. Table 10.4 gives the distribution of each income level reported according to whether or not a master's degree was held. As school-related income rises, the proportion of teachers who have a master's degree also rises. This does not hold true for non-school-related income. Both findings seem reasonable, since a teacher with advanced training should generally command a higher salary as a teacher but not necessarily in other areas of employment. As mentioned

Table 10.3
Income According to Hearing Status

Income	Hearing Impaired n	%	Not Hearing Impaired n	%	Total N	%
Non-School-Related						
None Reported	488	13.6	3112	86.4	3600	100.0
<$1,000	119	12.6	822	87.4	941	100.0
$1,000-1,999	31	19.2	130	80.7	161	100.0
$2,000-2,999	15	18.8	65	81.2	80	100.0
≥$3,000	30	24.0	95	76.0	125	100.0
School-Related						
None Reported	5	8.5	54	91.5	59	100.0
<$9,000	25	13.7	158	86.3	183	100.0
$9,000-9,999	20	7.3	255	92.7	275	100.0
$10,000-10,999	47	8.0	539	92.0	586	100.0
$11,000-11,999	86	13.0	573	86.9	659	100.0
$12,000-12,999	72	11.2	570	88.8	642	100.0
$13,000-13,999	81	15.1	454	84.8	535	100.0
$14,000-14,999	66	14.4	393	85.6	459	100.0
≥$15,000	261	17.5	1228	82.5	1489	100.0
All Subjects	663	13.6	4224	86.4	4887	100.0

before, many schools have a salary schedule based on education and experience. Table 10.4 reflects this fact.

Income also increases with years of teaching experience. This is true for both school-related and non-school-related

Table 10.4
Income According to Education

Income	Master's		No Master's		Total	
	n	%	n	%	N	%
Non-School-Related						
None Reported	2016	61.4	1264	38.5	3280	100.0
<$1,000	579	64.9	313	35.1	892	100.0
$1,000-1,999	114	74.5	39	25.5	153	100.0
$2,000-2,999	48	63.2	28	36.8	76	100.0
≧$3,000	83	69.7	36	30.3	119	100.0
School-Related						
None Reported	31	70.4	13	29.5	44	100.0
<$9,000	66	42.0	91	58.0	157	100.0
$9,000-9,999	57	28.2	145	71.8	202	100.0
$10,000-10,999	182	35.5	331	64.5	513	100.0
$11,000-11,999	313	52.5	283	47.5	596	100.0
$12,000-12,999	357	59.6	242	40.4	599	100.0
$13,000-13,999	340	66.4	172	33.6	512	100.0
$14,000-14,999	316	71.5	126	28.5	442	100.0
≧$15,000	1178	81.0	277	19.0	1455	100.0
All Subjects*	2840	62.8	1680	37.2	4520	100.0

*Note: This table does not include 367 cases who did not report whether they had a master's degree.

income. Table 10.5 gives the mean years of teaching experience reported by the respondents in each income category. The exception to the rule that more experience leads to higher salary is found among those who have a school-related income of less than $9,000. However, the number of teachers in this particular category is small, and most of them appeared to be special kinds of teachers (substitute teachers, older teachers with relatively little formal training, and so on).

Table 10.5
Income According to Years of Teaching Experience

Income	N	Mean Years of Experience
Non-School-Related		
None Reported	3357	9.0
<$1,000	885	7.1
$1,000-1,999	157	8.1
$2,000-2,999	74	9.4
≧$3,000	123	10.5
School-Related		
None Reported	41	13.6
<$9,000	154	8.2
$9,000-9,999	202	2.9
$10,000-10,999	501	3.5
$11,000-11,999	613	4.5
$12,000-12,999	618	6.2
$13,000-13,999	525	7.8
$14,000-14,999	456	9.7
≧$15,000	1486	13.7
All Subjects*	4596	8.6

*Note: This table does not include 291 subjects who did not report their total years of teaching experience.

It has been shown that education and experience both relate to reported income. Another point is that since teacher certification is related to professional qualifications, and since a more qualified teacher should command a higher income, it seems likely that the proportion of teachers holding teaching certificates should become larger as income increases. There is some evidence to support this hypothesis. Table 10.6 gives the percentages of teachers in each income group who hold CED and state teaching certificates. This table is abbreviated to save space and present only the salient facts. Non-school-related income is not reported in the table simply because there was no significant difference in certification among the non-school income categories. In Table 10.6, notice that the percentage of teachers holding certificates rises as income increases. This trend is somewhat clearer for state certification than for CED

Table 10.6
Percent at Each Income Level Who Hold CED and State Teaching Certificates

School-Related Income	% Holding CED Certificate	% Holding State Certificate
<$9,000	40.3	65.3
$9,000-9,999	44.2	77.3
$10,000-10,999	40.7	79.7
$11,000-11,999	44.1	82.5
$12,000-12,999	50.2	85.3
$13,000-13,999	56.0	83.8
$14,000-14,999	66.4	85.0
≥$15,000	55.8	88.1
All Subjects	48.5	81.8

certification, a finding which is to be expected, since salaries are usually set (or at least strongly influenced) by the state governments.

The data were also analyzed to determine whether a relationship existed between salary and academic level taught, and also between salary and type of teaching position held. No significant difference in salary was observed between the various academic levels, except that those who taught at the senior high level had a tendency to report slightly higher incomes. However, this appeared to reflect the earlier finding that those who teach at the senior high level tend to have a little more teaching experience.

Meaningful evaluation of the relationship between salary and kind of teaching position was difficult because out of the six categories, 75% of the respondents reported being class-room teachers. The only category which clearly commanded a higher salary was "supervising teacher," a finding which would be expected, since supervising teachers tend to have more education, experience, and responsibility. More than 60% of the 202 supervising teachers in this study reported school-related salaries of $15,000 or more, as compared with about 30% of the teachers in other categories.

Similarly, it was found that teachers who did not teach in a self-contained classroom received slightly higher salaries. Teachers who do not teach within self-contained classrooms often teach at the higher academic levels or may be special kinds of highly trained teachers. The point is that there are many variables in the data which seem to have some relationship to salary, but which actually represent different levels of training and experience. Training and experience appear to be the basic determiners of teacher income.

Eleven

Professional Affiliations

One measure of the professional activity of the teaching population in the education of the hearing impaired is the membership of teachers in organizations involved in professional services to teachers, hearing-impaired children and adults. There are many such organizations, ranging from large national groups to small community-service clubs. Table 11.1 gives the distribution of professional affiliations most commonly reported by the teachers in this study.

The organizations in Table 11.1 are ranked according to the frequency with which they were reported. The 26% in the "Other" category represents membership in a host of smaller organizations such as local teacher associations, local chapters of the National Education Association, the Delta Kappa educational organizations, vocational associations, and a number of professional associations not related to education of the hearing impaired.

The Convention of American Instructors of the Deaf (CAID) leads Table 11.1, closely followed by the National

Table 11.1
Distribution of Professional Affiliation

Organization	N*	% of 4887
Convention of American Instructors of the Deaf	1596	32.7
National Education Association	1472	30.1
Alexander Graham Bell Association for the Deaf	1009	20.6
Council for Exceptional Children	644	13.2
National Association of the Deaf	638	13.1
Registry of Interpreters for the Deaf	458	9.4
Gallaudet College Alumni Association	431	8.8
American Federation of Teachers	417	8.5
American Speech and Hearing Association	336	6.9
International Association of Parents of the Deaf	142	2.9
American Deafness and Rehabilitation Association	37	.8
Others	1255	25.7

*Note: Some respondents belonged to two or more organizations.

Education Association (NEA). The number of teachers who are members of the NEA and the American Federation of Teachers (AFT) is especially notable because these two organizations are strongly involved in issues related to various aspects of employment and employee benefits. Taken together, membership in the NEA and AFT is reported by almost 39% of the teaching population, a proportion which exceeds even that of the CAID. This seems to indicate a strong trend toward teacher participation in organizations concerned with the working conditions of teachers.

It is interesting to note that the Alexander Graham Bell Association for the Deaf (AGBAD) is reported by almost 21%

of the teachers while only 13% claim membership in the National Association of the Deaf (NAD). Although both organizations focus their activities on issues involving hearing impairment, the NAD has far greater support from the hearing-impaired people of this country. Perhaps the reason for the difference in proportion of teachers who are members of these two organizations is that the AGBAD is *for* the deaf while the NAD is *of* the deaf. This distinction is very clear among those teachers who are hearing-impaired. For this subgroup less than 10% are members of the AGBAD, but 45% are members of the NAD.

The membership differences between hearing and hearing-impaired teachers extend to other organizations. These differences are important because, to a limited extent, they provide some indication of the contrasting interests and priorities of hearing-impaired and hearing adults in the area of education of the hearing impaired. People tend to join organizations which reflect their views, and the prevailing views in these two groups do not always coincide.

Table 11.2 provides a breakdown of the professional affiliations for hearing and hearing-impaired teachers. Teachers who are hearing-impaired have a strong tendency to be members of the CAID (53%), the NAD (45%), and the Gallaudet College Alumni Association (GCAA) (54%). Since so many hearing-impaired teachers attended Gallaudet College, and since Gallaudet is primarily a college for the hearing impaired, the membership rate of the GCAA has relatively little meaning in the context of voluntary membership as discussed here. However, the rate of membership in the CAID and the NAD among teachers who are hearing-impaired clearly indicates very strong support for these two organizations, a support which is not matched by their hearing counterparts.

In contrast, the AGBAD, the Council for Exceptional Children (CEC), and the American Speech and Hearing Association (ASHA) have a lower rate of membership among

Table 11.2
Distributions of Professional Affiliations among Teachers Who Are Hearing and Hearing-Impaired

Organization	Hearing		Hearing-Impaired	
	N*	% of 4224	N*	% of 663
Convention of American Instructors of the Deaf	1242	29.4	354	53.4
National Education Association	1283	30.4	189	28.5
Alexander Graham Bell Association for the Deaf	946	22.4	63	9.5
Council for Exceptional Children	591	14.0	53	8.0
National Association of the Deaf	342	8.1	296	44.6
Registry of Interpreters for the Deaf	317	7.5	141	21.3
Gallaudet College Alumni Association	71	1.7	360	54.3
American Federation of Teachers	368	8.7	49	7.4
American Speech and Hearing Association	314	7.4	22	3.3
International Association of Parents of the Deaf	115	2.7	27	4.1
American Deafness and Rehabilitation Association	23	.5	14	2.1
Others	1097	26.0	158	23.8

*Note: Some respondents belonged to two or more organizations.

teachers who are hearing-impaired than among those who have normal hearing. Although no data is available in this study concerning the reasons why these organizations have lower membership rates among the hearing-impaired teachers, some general guesses can be hazarded. The AGBAD strongly advocates the use of speech and speechreading as the means of communication for the hearing impaired while many deaf people advocate the use of sign language within a philosophy of total communication. The CEC has a general interest in exceptional children and is not limited to the hearing impaired. ASHA is often thought to be more interested in the science of speech and audiology than in the broader social and educational aspects of hearing impairment. Perhaps these characteristics make the organizations of less interest to teachers who are hearing-impaired than to their hearing counterparts.

Overall, teachers who are hearing-impaired seem to have a greater tendency to join organizations related to their profession. The 663 teachers who were hearing-impaired reported 1,726 memberships, a 2.6 average. The 4,224 teachers who were not hearing-impaired reported 6,709 memberships, a 1.6 average.

The number of professional memberships seems to increase with age, regardless of hearing status. A comparison of teachers up to 30 years of age with those who were 31 or older revealed that the younger teachers belonged to an average of 1.5 organizations while the older teachers belonged to 1.9. The older teachers were more likely to be members of the CAID (40% versus 24%), the NEA (35% versus 25%), and the NAD (16% versus 10%). Further evidence of this is given in Table 11.3 but, as discussed earlier, this organization is a special case.

The general observation that the number of professional memberships increases with age is not surprising, but the fact that this increase seems to concentrate on three particular

Table 11.3
Mean Age and Years of Teaching Experience by Professional
Affiliations

Organization	Mean Age	Mean Experi- ence
Convention of American Instructors of the Deaf	36.6	10.8
National Education Association	35.2	9.6
Alexander Graham Bell Association for the Deaf	33.6	8.8
Council for Exceptional Children	33.6	8.4
National Association of the Deaf	35.9	9.6
Registry of Interpreters for the Deaf	35.0	9.7
Gallaudet College Alumni Association	39.2	12.0
American Federation of Teachers	34.4	9.3
American Speech and Hearing Association	34.0	9.2
International Association of Parents of the Deaf	35.6	9.1
American Deafness and Rehabilitation Association	33.1	7.9
Others	34.6	9.4

organizations has interesting implications. It may indicate that
these three groups offer something which makes membership
more attractive as teachers become older and gain experience.
Since it is known that membership of all three organizations
is rising, the larger proportion of older members is not simply
a case of not attracting new members from among young
teachers entering the field.

The professional affiliations reported in this study were
thought to vary according to the sex of the teachers also.
However, since 45% of the male teachers were hearing-

impaired, it was found that most of the differences in professional affiliations between males and females were actually attributable to hearing loss rather than sex. When teachers with hearing losses were excluded, differences according to sex were found only in membership to the CAID and AGBAD. Among the hearing males, 37% belonged to the CAID while only 28% of the hearing females reported membership. For the AGBAD, the percentages were 16% of the hearing males and 23% of the hearing females. All other organizations had no significant difference in membership according to sex. The mean number of affiliations reported was 1.6 for both males and females.

Twelve

Some Final Comments

The teachers of the hearing impaired in this study form a small subpopulation within the much larger population of all teachers in the United States. Although this subpopulation shares some characteristics with the larger group, there are also differences which clearly indicate its uniqueness.

Perhaps the best way to highlight the uniqueness of the teachers in this study is to compare the data with similar data published by the National Education Association (NEA). The NEA's most recent survey of teachers (Reams, 1977) was carried out during the 1975-76 school year and involved a random sample of 1,374 teachers employed in public school systems across the country.

First, teachers of the hearing impaired (T-HI) appeared to be slightly younger than teachers in public schools (T-PS).

Note: A longer version of this chapter first appeared in American Annals of the Deaf, *1980,* 124, *1. The authors thank the journal for permission to reprint that material here.*

Among the T-HI group, 75% were under 40 years of age, as compared with 67% of the T-PS group. Further, the T-HI had a greater proportion of female teachers than the T-PS (83% versus 67%). Possibly because of their younger age, a smaller per- centage of the T-HI were married (61% versus 71%) and had children (38% versus 55%). For both the T-HI and T-PS groups, the proportion of teachers who were members of a minority ethnic group (5% and 8%, respectively) was far below the proportion in the general population.

Both groups were well educated with 97% of the T-HI sample and 99% of the T-PS sample reporting that they had earned a bachelor's degree. However, teachers of the hearing impaired are highly specialized and are usually required to have training beyond the level needed to teach normal hearing chil- dren. This is probably the reason why 75% of the T-HI reported having a master's degree, as compared to only 37% of the T-PS.

The teaching environment in which teachers of the hearing impaired and public school teachers function is very different in some respects. The most obvious and visible difference is class size. The average public school teacher reported classes of 25 students while most teachers of the hearing impaired reported six students in their classes. Both groups usually taught between 180 and 184 days per year, but the level of teaching and the content of the courses show a different emphasis. Teachers of the hearing impaired appeared to be more flexible and to teach at more than one level, with a concentration in the lower grades. In contrast, public school teachers appeared to be more evenly distributed among the various grades and to be individually responsible for a narrower range of courses.

The differences between the teaching environments of the two groups seemed to stem directly from the fact that teachers of the hearing impaired must constantly function as teachers of language and communication. They are faced with a more technically complex teaching task, one which requires a high level of specialized training in a variety of areas and demands both innovation and flexibility.

In spite of their greater professional training and more complex teaching task, there was little evidence in the data to suggest that teachers of the hearing impaired commanded a higher salary. The median salary of the T-HI was $13,000 for the 1978-79 school year. The T-PS reported a median salary of $11,300 for the 1975-76 school year. Allowing a 5% cost of living increase for each of the three years from 1976 to 1979, the adjusted median salary of the T-PS was $13,000, the same for the T-HI.

Although this has been only a brief overview of an extensive and complex file of data, it has clearly shown that teachers of the hearing impaired are a unique subpopulation with distinct demographic characteristics which distinguish it from the larger population of public school teachers. Teachers of the hearing impaired work in a special environment and are required to possess special skills to teach a special group of children in special ways. Further analysis of the data in this study and additional investigation by other researchers should lead to a better understanding of this selected group of educators.

Reference Notes

1. Desmond, M. Medical aspects of the congenital rubella syndrome. Paper presented at the Baylor College of Medicine, Houston, July, 1975.
2. Schildroth, A. Personal communication. Office of Demographic Studies, Gallaudet College, Washington, D.C., 1980.

References

Abeson, A., & Fleury, J. (Eds.) State certification requirements for education of the handicapped. In J. Gilmore & N. Argyros, *Special education certification: A state of the art survey.* New York: The Research Foundation of the City University of New York, 1977.

Babbidge, H. *Education of the deaf in the United States.* Washington, D.C.: U.S. Government Printing Office, 1965.

Bender, R. *The conquest of deafness.* Cleveland: Case Western Reserve, 1970.

Brill, R. *Administrative and professional developments in the education of the deaf.* Washington, D.C.: Gallaudet College Press, 1971.

Brill, R. *The training of academic teachers of the deaf.* Unpublished doctoral dissertation, Rutgers University, 1950.

Brill, R., Merrill, E., & Frisina, R. *Recommended organizational policies in the education of the deaf.* Washington, D.C.: The Conference of Executives of American Schools for the Deaf, Incorporated, 1973.

Carey, H. Legislation and education of the deaf. In S. Silverman (Ed.), *Education of the deaf: The challenge and the charge.* Washington, D.C.: U.S. Government Printing Office, 1968.

Conference of Executives of American Schools for the Deaf, Incorporated. Definition of total communication. In I. Jordan, G. Gustason, & R. Rosen. Current communication trends at programs for the deaf. *American Annals of the Deaf,* 1976, *121*, 6.

Council on Education of the Deaf. *Standards for the certification of teachers of the hearing impaired.* Washington, D.C.: Council on Education of the Deaf, 1972.

Craig, W., & Craig, H. (Eds.) Reference issue. *American Annals of the Deaf,* 1978, *123*, 2.

Davis, H., & Silverman, S. (Eds.) *Hearing and deafness* (3rd ed.). New York: Holt, Rinehart, and Winston, 1970.

General Accounting Office. *Training educators for the handicapped: A need to redirect federal programs.* Washington, D.C.: U.S. Congress, 1976.

Gilmore, J., & Argyros, N. *Special education certification: A state of the art survey.* New York: The Research Foundation of the City University of New York, 1977.

Hall, P. A plan for certification of teachers. *American Annals of the Deaf,* 1931, *76,* 4.

Jensema, C. Three characteristics of teachers of the deaf who are hearing impaired. *American Annals of the Deaf,* 1977, *122,* 3.

Jensema, C., & Trybus, R. *Communication patterns and educational achievement of hearing impaired students* (Series T2). Washington, D.C.: Office of Demographic Studies, Gallaudet College, 1978.

Jordan, I., Gustason, G., & Rosen, R. Current communication trends at programs for the deaf. *American Annals of the Deaf,* 1976, *121,* 6.

Long, J. The certification of teachers. *American Annals of the Deaf,* 1931, *76,* 4.

Maile, R. Certification requirements for teachers of the deaf: A study of state requirements and their relationship to the certification standards of the Council on Education of the Deaf. *American Annals of the Deaf,* 1978, *123,* 8.

Moores, D. *Educating the deaf: Psychology, principles and practices.* Boston: Houghton Mifflin Company, 1978.

Proceedings of the Fourteenth Conference of Superintendents and Principals of American Schools for the Deaf. *American Annals of the Deaf,* 1929, *74,* 2.

Rawlings, B., & Trybus, R. Personnel, facilities, and services available in schools and classes for hearing impaired children in the United States. *American Annals of the Deaf,* 1978, *123,* 2.

Schein, J., & Delk, M. *The deaf population in the United States.* Silver Spring, MD: The National Association of the Deaf, 1974.

Silverman, S. (Ed.) *Education of the deaf: The challenge and the charge.* Washington, D.C.: U.S. Government Printing Office, 1968.

Talbot, B. Changes in our profession. *American Annals of the Deaf,* 1895, *40,* 3.

Appendix A

Cover Letter to Program Administrators

GALLAUDET COLLEGE
KENDALL GREEN, WASHINGTON, D.C. 20002

Department of Administration

October 6, 1978

Dear Administrator,

We would like to ask your assistance in obtaining information for a study which is being conducted through the Department of Administration at Gallaudet College. This study is an attempt to statistically describe the characteristics of the population of teachers in special education programs for the hearing impaired throughout the United States. It is hoped that the results of the study will find many uses, especially in the area of educational planning.

Enclosed is a packet of forms pertaining to teacher characteristics. Would you please give one form to each of your teachers who are actively teaching either full or part time during the 1978-1979 school year and have them take a few minutes to fill it out? They should return their forms directly to us in the postage paid envelopes provided.

All information collected will be kept confidential. The forms do not request the names of either the teachers or the school.

A copy of the resulting monograph will be forwarded to your educational program for your perusal after this study is completed.

When you have completed distributing the forms, please indicate on the attached reply card the number of teachers who received a form. Also, please indicate the number of additional forms you may need. Mail the postcard to us at your earliest convenience. Let us assure you that at no time will responses be traceable to an individual.

Sincerely,

EDWARD E. CORBETT, JR., M.A.
Doctoral Candidate

CARL J. JENSEMA, Ph.D.
Assistant Professor
Chairman of Dissertation Committee

Doctoral Committee:

DOIN E. HICKS, Ed.D.
Professor

THOMAS A. MAYES, Ph.D.
Associate Professor
Chairman of Doctoral Committee

EDMOND J. SKINSKI, Ed.D.
Associate Professor

MICHAEL L. SUPLEY, Ed.D.
Assistant Professor

Cover Letter to Teachers and the Study Instrument

GALLAUDET COLLEGE

KENDALL GREEN, WASHINGTON, D.C. 20002

Department of Administration

October 6, 1978

Dear Colleague,

We are asking you, and 12,000 other teachers of the hearing impaired, to participate in a nation-wide study in order to obtain certain information about this teaching population. Your responses to the questions on the following pages are extremely important to the study's validity. The information will be used for statistical purposes only, and no individual teacher or school will be identified. Confidentiality of your answers is absolutely guaranteed.

It is our sincere hope that you will agree to participate. The more teachers who respond, the more accurate the information base will be and ultimately, the more the study will benefit teachers of the hearing impaired.

When this study is completed, a copy of the resulting monograph will be forwarded to your educational program for your perusal.

Please answer all questions to the best of your ability. Please fill out the form as soon as possible and no later than October 31, 1978. Return it directly to us in the attached, postage paid and addressed envelope.

Sincerely,

EDWARD E. CORBETT, JR., M.A.
    Doctoral Candidate

CARL J. JENSEMA, Ph.D.
    Assistant Professor
    Chairman of Dissertation Committee

Doctoral Committee:

DOIN E. HICKS, Ed.D.
    Professor

THOMAS A. MAYES, Ph.D.
    Associate Professor
    Chairman of Doctoral Committee

EDMOND J. SKINSKI, Ed.D.
    Associate Professor

MICHAEL L. SUPLEY, Ed.D.
    Assistant Professor

A DESCRIPTIVE STUDY OF TEACHERS OF THE HEARING IMPAIRED IN THE UNITED STATES

DEPARTMENT OF ADMINISTRATION
GALLAUDET COLLEGE
WASHINGTON, D.C. 20002

DIRECTIONS: This study is being conducted in order to obtain certain information about the teaching population in the education of the hearing impaired. Your answers will be kept confidential. The information will be used for statistical purposes only, and no individual person or school will be identified. Please answer all questions to the best of your ability.

PERSONAL:

Birthdate: _____   Sex: ☐ Male   ☐ Female
Month   Day   Year

Marital Status: ☐ Single   ☐ Married   ☐ Widowed   ☐ Divorced/Separated

Number of Children: _____

Ethnic Background: ☐ White   ☐ Black   ☐ Spanish American   ☐ Oriental   ☐ American Indian

☐ Other (specify): _____

EDUCATION:

UNDERGRADUATE: Name(s) of College/University attended: _____

Do you have a Bachelor's degree? ☐ Yes   ☐ No   If Yes, year graduated _____ Major: _____

GRADUATE: Name(s) of College/University attended: _____

Do you have a Master's degree? ☐ Yes   ☐ No   If Yes, year graduated _____ Major: _____

What other formal education and/or degrees do you have? _____
_____

Did you receive financial assistance during your training as a teacher of the hearing impaired? ☐ Yes   ☐ No

If Yes, source: _____

Last University/College credit earned: 19_____

CERTIFICATION:

Do you hold a CED/CEASD teaching certificate? ☐ Yes   ☐ No

If "Yes"; is this certificate: ☐ Provisional   ☐ Professional

Since 1972 CED/CEASD has been issuing certificates in six major teaching specialities. Please check your major specialty and the appropriate sub-specialty in which you are certified.

☐ Preprimary	☐ Secondary (academic area)	☐ Secondary (special subject area)	☐ Special Content Areas
☐ Infant	☐ Mathematics	☐ Business Science	☐ Art
☐ Nursery	☐ Science	☐ Home Economics	☐ Library Science
	☐ History	☐ Industrial Arts	☐ Media
☐ Elementary	☐ Social Studies	☐ Graphic Arts	☐ Speech
☐ Multihandicapped	☐ English	☐ Other: _____	☐ Physical Education
	☐ Other: _____		☐ Other: _____

Do you hold a **State** teaching certificate in Special Education? ☐ Yes   ☐ No

If "Yes," name of State: _____   Area of specialization: _____

Type of certificate: ☐ Standard   ☐ Advanced   ☐ Provisional   ☐ Other (specify): _____

What other teaching certificates do you hold? _____

PROFESSIONAL AFFILIATIONS:

Which of these national organizations do you belong to?

☐ Convention of American Instructors of the Deaf

☐ Alexander Graham Bell Association for the Deaf

☐ American Speech and Hearing Association

☐ National Association of the Deaf

☐ National Education Association

☐ American Federation of Teachers

☐ Other (please specify): _____

☐ The Council for Exceptional Children

☐ International Association of Parents of the Deaf

☐ Gallaudet College Alumni Association

☐ The Registry of Interpreters for the Deaf

☐ American Deafness and Rehabilitation Association

TEACHING EXPERIENCE:

Are you presently employed as a:

☐ Supervising Teacher ☐ Regular Teacher (Full-Time) ☐ Resource Teacher ☐ Substitute Teacher (Part-Time)

☐ Itinerant Teacher ☐ Other (specify): _____

How many years have you taught? _____ Total years

How many years have you taught in each of these environments?

_____ Education of the Hearing Impaired _____ Other Special Education _____ General Education

How many years have you taught in your present educational program (including the 1978-1979 school year)? _____ years

What level(s) do you presently teach? ☐ Preschool ☐ Elementary ☐ Middle ☐ Senior High ☐ Other: _____

Are you teaching in a self-contained classroom? ☐ Yes ☐ No

How many days during the 1978-1979 school year are you required to teach? _____ days

What subjects do you presently teach? (Please check the appropriate boxes.)

☐ Language ☐ Social Studies ☐ Science

☐ Reading ☐ Driver's Education ☐ Physical Education

☐ Communication ☐ History ☐ Prevocational (specify): _____

☐ Mathematics ☐ Art ☐ Elective(s) (specify): _____

What is the average number of students you have in **each** of your classes this year? _____ students

What is the age range of your students this year? _____ to _____ years old.

What extra-curricular activities do you supervise in your school? _____

SALARY: (This information is necessary for comparing the income of teachers with the income of people in other professions. Your responses will be very strictly confidential.)

Please check the total **school-related** salary you are now receiving to the nearest thousand dollar mark:

☐ $ 8,999 or less ☐ $12,000 - 12,999

☐ $ 9,000 - 9,999 ☐ $13,000 - 13,999

☐ $10,000 - 10,999 ☐ $14,000 - 14,999

☐ $11,000 - 11,999 ☐ $15,000 or more

Please check the total **non-school-related** salary you are now receiving to the nearest thousand dollar mark:

☐ $ 999 or less

☐ $1,000 - 1,999

☐ $2,000 - 2,999

☐ $3,000 or more

COMMUNICATION:

Most teachers use some **combination** of communication methods in communicating to their students. In the space below please try to estimate how much of **each** communication mode you usually use in your classroom interaction. Check the box which most closely estimates the percentage of time you use **each** mode. (Your total percentage of all modes will probably exceed 100%.)

	Seldom 0-25%	Sometimes 26-50%	Usually 51-75%	Always 76-100%
Cued Speech	☐	☐	☐	☐
Speech	☐	☐	☐	☐
Manual Signs and Fingerspelling (both Ameslan and Signed English)	☐	☐	☐	☐
Fingerspelling only	☐	☐	☐	☐
Gestures	☐	☐	☐	☐
Writing	☐	☐	☐	☐
Other (specify): _____	☐	☐	☐	☐

Rate how well you **speechread**:	Rate how well people **speechread** you:	Rate your **sign** communication skills:		Rate your **fingerspelling** communication skills:	
		Expressive	**Receptive**	**Expressive**	**Receptive**
☐ Very Good	☐ Very Good	☐ Very Good	☐ Very Good	☐ Very Good	☐ Very Good
☐ Good	☐ Good	☐ Good	☐ Good	☐ Good	☐ Good
☐ Fair	☐ Fair	☐ Fair	☐ Fair	☐ Fair	☐ Fair
☐ Poor	☐ Poor	☐ Poor	☐ Poor	☐ Poor	☐ Poor
☐ Cannot Speechread	☐ Cannot be Speechread	☐ Cannot Sign	☐ Cannot Read Signs	☐ Cannot Fingerspell	☐ Cannot Read Fingerspelling

What is the average number of hours per week you spend with **deaf** people in activities **not** related to your job? _____ hours

What is the average number of hours per week you spend with **hearing** people in activities **not** related to your job? _____ hours

HANDICAPPING CONDITIONS:

Do you have any of the following conditions?

☐ Cerebral Palsy
☐ Orthopedic
☐ Epilepsy
☐ Heart Disorder
☐ Severe Visual Loss
☐ Hearing Loss
☐ Other (please specify): _____

Are any of the following people in **your** family hearing impaired?

	Yes	No	If "yes," how many?
Spouse	☐	☐	_____
Children	☐	☐	_____
Parents	☐	☐	_____
Siblings	☐	☐	_____
Grandparents	☐	☐	_____
Other (specify):			
_____	☐	☐	_____

IF YOU DO NOT HAVE A HEARING LOSS, SKIP THE REMAINDER OF THIS QUESTIONNAIRE.

HEARING STATUS:

Age at onset of hearing loss: _____ years   ☐ At Birth   ☐ Unknown

What is your unaided hearing loss in the better ear?

☐ Normal Limits (Less than 27 dB, ISO)   ☐ Moderately Severe (56-70 dB, ISO)
☐ Mild (27-40 dB, ISO)   ☐ Severe (71-90 dB, ISO)
☐ Moderate (41-55 dB, ISO)   ☐ Profound (91 dB plus, ISO)

What is the cause of your hearing loss?

☐ Maternal Rubella   ☐ Prematurity   ☐ Mumps   ☐ Accident
☐ Trauma at Birth   ☐ Rh Incompatibility   ☐ Infections   ☐ Cause Cannot Be Determined
☐ Other Complications of Pregnancy   ☐ Meningitis   ☐ Measles   ☐ Other (please specify):
☐ Heredity   ☐ High Fever   ☐ Otitis Media   _____

Do you wear a hearing aid? ☐ Yes   ☐ No

Without a hearing aid is your discrimination of normal conversational speech:	**With** a hearing aid is your discrimination of normal conversational speech:	In speaking to a stranger who has normal hearing would you rate your speech intelligibility as:
☐ Normal	☐ Normal	☐ Normal
☐ Good	☐ Good	☐ Good
☐ Fair	☐ Fair	☐ Fair
☐ Poor	☐ Poor	☐ Poor
☐ Cannot discriminate any speech	☐ Cannot discriminate any speech	☐ Not intelligible

For your childhood education, how many years did you attend each of the following program types:

_____ Residential School for the Deaf   _____ Public School Special Education Classes for the Deaf

_____ Day School for the Deaf   _____ Public School Regular Classes

_____ Other (explain): _____

Complete Listing of Educational Programs Serving the Hearing Impaired in the United States

Alabama

Alabama School for the Deaf
Auburn City Schools
Bessemer Board of Education
Birmingham Public Schools
Huntsville City Schools
Children's Center—Montgomery
Etowah County Board of Education
Holt Elementary School
Huntsville Rehabilitation Center
Lewis-Slossfield Speech and Hearing
Mobile County Schools
Mobile Preschool for the Deaf
University of Montevallo Speech and Hearing Center
Northwest Alabama Rehabilitation Center
The Shrine School
Springhill Preschool Church
Striplin Elementary
Tuscaloosa Preschool for the Deaf Class
West Athens Elementary

Alaska

Alaska Treatment Center
Alaska Program for the Deaf
Fairbanks North Star Borough

Arizona

Arizona School for the Deaf
Arizona Training Program at Coolidge
Easter Seal Society Preschool Program
Glendale Union High School District
Holdeman School, Tempe School District
Madison School District #38
Mesa Public Schools
Phoenix Day School
Phoenix Elementary School District #1
Phoenix Union High School District
Samuel Gompers Rehabilitation Center
Scottsdale Unified School District #48
Sierra Vista Preschool
Tucson Public Schools
Washington Elementary District #6

Arkansas

Arkansas School for the Deaf
Arkansas Children's Colony
Arkansas School for the Blind
Arkansas Children's Hearing and Speech Center
Children's House of Learning
Fayetteville Public Schools
Jenkins Memorial Children's Center
Little Rock Public Schools

Source: Office of Demographic Studies, Gallaudet College, Washington, D.C. 20002

Pulaski County Special School
District

California

California School for the Deaf at
Fremont

California School for the Deaf at
Riverside

California School for the Blind

Fairview State Hospital

Sonoma State Hospital School
District

Porterville Hearing Handicapped
Program

Alameda County Hearing Impaired
Program

Alhambra City and High School
District

Alum Rock Union Elementary
School District

Anaheim Union High School
District

Compton Unified School District

Barstow Unified School District

Bellflower Unified School District

Mary Bennett School for the Deaf

Birmingham High School

Butte County Special Education
Unit

Calvert Street School

Carlsbad Unified School District

Cedarcreek School for the Hearing
Impaired

Center for Exceptional Children

Centralia School District

Ceres Unified School District

Sierra Sands Unified School
District

Chula Vista City School District

Clay Junior High School

Covina Valley Unified School
District

Contra Costa County Schools

Cutler-Orosi Unified School District

East San Gabriel Valley School

El Centro School District

El Dorado City Schools

Escondido Union Elementary
School District

Escondido Union High School
District

Eureka City School

Fremont Union High School
District

John Blacow Elementary School

Fresno City Unified School District

Gardena High School

Garden Grove Unified School
District

Glendale Unified School District

Goleta Union School District

Grossmont Union High School
District

Hayward Unified School District

Hanford Elementary School
District

Harbor Educational Unit

Hi Desert Oral School

Hollywood High School

Humbolt County Schools

Jefferson Elementary School
District

Kennedy Children's Center

Kern County Schools

La Mesa-Spring Valley School
District

Lancaster Special Educational
District

La Conte Junior High School

Little Lake City Elementary School District

West Valley School

Lompoc Unified School District

Long Beach Unified School District

153rd Street School

Los Angeles City Unified School District

Madera County Schools

Marin County Schools

Marlton School

Melrose Avenue School

Mesa Vista Hearing and Language Center

Merced County Department of Education

Monache High School

Montebello Unified School District

Monterey County Schools

Mt. Diablo Unified School District

Mulholland Junior High School

Napa Valley Unified School District

Newport-Mesa Unified School District

Norwalk-La Mirada Unified School District

Oakland Unified School District

Ocean View School District

Oral Education Center of Southern California

Oralingua School for the Hearing Impaired

Orange County Educational Assessment Center

Orange Unified School District

Orcutt Union School District

Pajard Valley Unified School District

Palo Alto Unified School District

Pittsburg Unified School District

Placentia Unified School District

Pomona Unified School District

Pasadena Unified School District

Peninsula Oral School

Placer County—Newcastle School

Project IDEA

Redwood City Schools

Richmond Unified School District

Riverside County Association

Riverside County Schools

Riverside Unified School District

Sacramento City Unified School District

St. Joseph's School for the Deaf

Salvin Elementary School

San Bernardino County Schools

San Diego Speech and Hearing Center

San Diego Unified School District

San Francisco Hearing and Speech Center

San Francisco County Unified School District

San Jose City Unified School District

San Juan Unified School District

San Luis Obispo County Office of Education

San Mateo Union High School District

San Mateo County Class for the Deaf

Santa Ana School District

Santa Clara School District

Santa Cruz School District

Santa Monica Unified School District

Santa Rosa City School District

Saticoy School

SELACO-Downey

Shasta County Schools

Simi Valley Unified School District

Solano County Aurally Handicapped

Southwest School for the Deaf

Stockton Unified School District

Sunnyvale Elementary School District

Sutter County-Lincrest

Tehama County Schools

Tustin Unified School District

The John Tracy Clinic

Tulare County Schools

Tuolumne County Schools

Union School District—Oster School

Vallejo City Unified School District

Ventura Unified School District

White Point School

Newport-Mesa Deaf/Hard of Hearing Program

Colorado

Colorado School for the Deaf

Adams County Consolidated School District

Aurora Public Schools

Greeley Public Schools

Boulder Valley Public Schools

Central Elementary—Commerce City

School District #1

Children's Hospital

Colorado Springs Public School District #11

Denver Public Schools

Fitzsimons General Hospital

Jefferson Unified School District

School District #6—Littleton

Mesa County Valley School District #51

Poudre R-1 School District

Pueblo School District #60

St. Vrain Valley Public Schools

University of Denver Speech and Hearing Center

Colorado Hearing and Speech at Adams County

Porter Hospital, Adams County

Connecticut

American School for the Deaf

Oak Hill School

Blackham School

Capitol Region Educational Council

East Fairfield County Rehabilitation Center

East Hartford Public Schools

Easter Seal—Goodwill

Hamden-New Haven Cooperative Educational Services

Hartford Board of Education

Prudence Crandall School

Middletown Public Schools

Norwalk Board of Education

New Britain Public Schools

Fairfield Public Schools

Area Cooperative Educational Services

Stamford Public Schools

Village St. School (Green Acres)

Watertown Public Schools

Weathersfield Public Schools

East Rock Community Schools

Delaware

The Margaret S. Sterck School for the Hearing Impaired

Wilmington Public Schools

District of Columbia

Children's Hospital

D.C. Public Schools, Department of Special Education

D.C. Public Schools, Pupil Personnel Services

Kendall Demonstration Elementary School

Model Secondary School for the Deaf

Washington Hearing Society

Florida

Florida School for the Deaf

Sunland Training Center

Alachua County Schools

All Children's Speech and Hearing Clinic

Bay County School Board

Brevard County Schools

Broward County Schools

Dade County Public Schools

Duval County Schools

Easter Seal Rehabilitation Center

Escambia County Schools

Fort Lauderdale Oral School

Grant School of Miami, Incorporated

Hillsborough County Public Schools

Hobbs Middle School

Speech and Hearing Center, Incorporated—Jackson

Lee County Special Education

Leon County Program for Hearing Impaired

Robert McCord Oral School

Manatee County Schools

Okaloosa County Schools

Orange County Public Schools

Palm Beach County Schools

Pinellas County Schools

School Board of Polk County

Robinson Elementary School

Sarasota County Schools

Shaw Kindergarten Center

Tampa Oral School

Tri-County Deaf Program

University of Florida Speech and Hearing Clinic

Aural Rehabilitation Program at the University of Miami

Volusia County Hearing Impaired Program

Georgia

Georgia School for the Deaf

Davison School, Incorporated

Georgia Academy for the Blind

Atlanta Area School for the Deaf

Atlanta Speech School

Atlanta Public Schools

Cherokee County Schools

Clarke County Schools

Clayton County Schools

Cobb County Board of Education

Dalton City Schools

DeKalb County Program

Dooly County Schools

Douglas County Board of Education

Forest Hills Elementary School

Georgia Easter Seal Speech and Hearing Center

Weed Elementary School

Fitzgerald City Schools

Franklin and Hart County Programs

Fulton County Special Education Office

Georgia Center for the Multi-Handicapped

Gilmer County Board of Education

Speech and Hearing Clinic, Gracewood

Houston Speech School

Listening Eyes School

Moultrie Speech and Hearing Center

Muscogee County Schools

Oak Hill Center

Georgia Program for Exceptional Children

Savannah Public Schools

Savannah Speech and Hearing Center

Southwest Georgia Easter Seal Rehabilitation Center

Spalding-Griffin County Schools

T.C. Tinsley School—Special Education Center

Valdosta Public Schools

Central Georgia Speech and Hearing Center, Baldwin

Hawaii

Hawaii School for the Deaf and the Blind

Honaunau Elementary School

Kahala Elementary School

Kauai High and Intermediate Schools

Lehua Elementary School

McKinley High School

Pearl Harbor Kai Elementary

Sultan Easter Seal School

Wainae School

Washington Intermediate School

Wilcox Elementary School

Idaho

Idaho School for the Deaf

Idaho State University Speech and Hearing Clinic

Ramsay Training School

School District #91

JSD #215—Fremont County

Illinois

Illinois School for the Deaf

Dixon State School

Elim Christian School

Illinois School for the Visually Impaired

Illinois Children's Hospital School

Lincoln State School

Banneker School

Alexander Graham Bell School

Moline Hearing Handicapped Program

Catholic Charities

Chicago Vocational High School

Chicago Board of Education

Drew School

Ericson School

Evanston Community School District

Evanston Township High School

Franklin School

R. Graham School of Special Education

Greene Elementary

Harrison High School

Holy Trinity Day Class

Holy Trinity High School

Illinois State Pediatric Institute

Illinois State University Day Class for the Deaf

Institute for Hearing and Speech

Jamieson School

Educational Regional Association (Joliet)

Lake-McHenry Regional Program for the Hearing Impaired

Lake View High School

Lane Technical High School

Marquette School

Morrill School

North Suburban Special Education District

Northwestern Illinois Association

N-Northwest Program for the Hearing Impaired Children

Perry School

Quincy Public Schools

Reinberg School

Ray School

Rockford Public Schools

St. Mary's of Perpetual Care

St. Joseph Hospital

Scammon School

Schurz High School

Shields School

Siegel Institute for Communicative Disorders

South Metropolitian Association

Spalding High School

Springfield Public School District #186

James Ward Elementary School

Southern Illinois Regional Program for the Hearing Impaired

Whitney M. Young High School

Ella Flagg Young School

Southwestern Regional Program Special Education Association

East Central Regional Program at Champaign

West Suburban Association for the Hearing Handicapped—Cook County

Mid-Central Association

Indiana

Indiana School for the Deaf

Fort Wayne State Training Center and Hospital

Bahr School (Central State Hospital)

Allen County Society for Crippled Children

Anderson Oral Deaf Class

Ball State University

Coordinating Center for Rehabilitation

Cross Road Rehabilitation Center

Hammond Public Schools

Elkhart Community Schools

Elkhart Rehabilitation Center

Rehabilitation Center—Evansville

Fayette County School Corporation

Fort Wayne Community Schools

Gary Community Schools

Evansville-Vanderburg School Corporation

Green Acres School

Indianapolis Public Schools

Indianapolis Speech and Hearing Center

Lafayette School Corporation

Logansport Special Education, Hearing Impaired Program

Marion Community Schools

Michigan City Area Schools

Monroe County Community Schools

Monroe County Preschool

Muncie Community Schools

New Albany-Floyd County Oral Program

Northwest Indiana Special Education Cooperative

Plymouth Community School Corporation

Porter County Special Education Cooperative

Purdue University Department of Audiology and Speech Services

Hearing and Speech Center—St. Joseph County

Southbend Community School Corporation

Southeast Indiana Rehabilitation Center

Trade Winds Rehabilitation Center

Vigo County Schools

Anthony Wayne Rehabilitation Center

Iowa

Iowa School for the Deaf

Arrowhead Educational Agency

Area Educational Agency #6

Area Educational Agency #7

Cedar Rapids Community Schools

Grant Wood Area Educational Agency

Des Moines Infant-Preschool Program

Faith School

Glenwood State Hospital School

Green Valley Area Educational Agency #14

Hope Haven

Dubuque County Program for the Hearing Impaired

Area Educational Agency #11

Sioux City Community School District

Siouxland Rehabilitation Center

Taylor Elementary Rehabilitation Center

Wapello County School System

Wilson Oral Deaf Department

Mississippi Bend Area Educational Agency

B. Vista Cher Craw Ida County School

Kansas

Kansas School for the Deaf

Institute of Logopedics

Lakemary Center

Parsons State Hospital and Training Center

Reno Regional Educational Services

Lawrence-Grant Unified School District #497

Shawnee Mission Public Schools

Topeka Public Schools

Mark Twain School—Wyandotte Special Education Cooperative

University of Kansas Medical Center

Heusner Elementary

Unified School District #383

Dodge City Unified School District #431

Unified School District #443

Wichita Public Schools

Kentucky

Kentucky School for the Deaf

Bowling Green Independent Schools

Central Elementary School

Covington Independent Schools

Fayette County Schools

Harrison County Board of Education

Jefferson County Public Schools

Easter Seal Society Hearing and Speech Center

Lexington Deaf Oral Department

Louisville Public Schools

Louisville Deaf Oral School

Marion County Independent School District

Sayre School

Western Kentucky Easter Seal Center

Cooper School

Louisiana

Louisiana School for the Deaf

Louisiana State School for the Deaf—Southern Branch

Acadia Parish School Board

Baton Rouge Speech and Hearing Foundation

Chinchuba Institute for the Deaf

The Bright Preschool for the Hearing Impaired

Crippled Children's Hospital

Eden Gardens Oral School

Hilde Knopf School for the Deaf

Jefferson Parish Schools

Lafayette Parish Schools

Monroe City Schools

New Orleans Public Schools

Northwestern State University Laboratory School

Pinecrest State School

Speech and Hearing Center of Southwestern Louisiana

Sunset Acres School for the Hearing Impaired

Terrebonne Parish Schools

T.H. Watkins Elementary School

Maine

The Governor Baxter School for the Deaf

Pineland Center

Bangor Regional Speech and Hearing Center

Lake Region High School

Northeast Hearing and Speech Center

Pine Tree Society

Mary Snow School

Thayer Hospital

University of Maine Speech and Hearing—Ardostock

Maryland

Maryland School for the Deaf, Frederick

Maryland School for the Deaf, Columbia

Glenn-Dale Hospital

Rosewood State Hospital

Anne Arundel County Schools

Baltimore City Public Schools

Baltimore County Schools

Carroll County Board of Education

Dorchester County Hearing Impaired Programs

Gateway Preschool for the Hearing Impaired

Harford County Board of Education

Kent County Board of Education

Montgomery County Public Schools

Prince George's County Public Schools

St. Mary's County Board of Education

Talbot County Board of Education

Washington County Board of Education

Massachusetts

Beverly School for the Deaf

Boston School for the Deaf

Clarke School for the Deaf

Perkins School for the Blind

Woburn Day Classes

Bethany Hill School for the Multi-Handicapped

Boston College Campus School

Blue Hills Program for the Hearing Impaired

Brockton Public Schools

Canton Rehabilitation Center

Children's Hospital Medical Center

Concord Public Schools

Paul A. Dever School

Duxbury Program for the Hearing Impaired Children

Fall River Day Classes

Hogan Regional Center

Kennedy Memorial Hospital for Children

Lawrence Public Schools

The Learning Center for Deaf Children

Leominster-Lincoln School

The Little People School

Lowell Preschool for the Deaf

Jackson-Mann School

Keefe Technical High School

North Shore Special Education Consortium

New Bedford Schools

Edco Secondary Educational Program

Parmenter School District

Reading Day Classes for the Deaf

Willie Ross School for the Deaf

Somerset Habilitation Center

Springfield Day Class for the Deaf

Stoughton Public Schools

Taunton Public Schools

Thayer-Lindsley Nursery

Worcester Public Schools

Waltham Public Schools

Wellfleet Day Class

Whittier Regional Vocational Technical High School

Worcester County Hearing and Speech Center

Michigan

Michigan School for the Deaf
Lutheran School
Michigan School for the Blind
Allen Park Public Schools
Ann Arbor Public Schools
Battle Creek Public Schools
Bay-Arenac Intermediate School District
Bloomfield Hills Public Schools
Branch County Intermediate School District
Brighton Area Schools
Constantine Public Schools
Copper County Intermediate School District
Dearborn Public Schools
Detroit Day School for the Deaf
Garden City Public Schools
Durant-Tuuri-Mott School
Eastern Michigan University
Escanaba Oral School
City of Ferndale School District
Saginaw Board of Education
Hillsdale Intermediate School District
Holland Public Schools
Ida Public Schools
Ionia County Intermediate School District
Delta Schoolcraft Intermediate School District
Jackson Public Schools
Kalamazoo Public Schools
Kent Intermediate School District
Lakeview Public Schools
Lansing School District
Lapeer School

Mary McGuire School
Muskegon Public Schools
Marquette-Alger Intermediate School District
Oakland Public Schools
Charlevoix-Emmet Intermediate School District
City of Pontiac School District
Port Huron Area Public School District
Program for Hearing Impaired Babies
Redford Union Schools
Shawnee Public Schools
Shiawassee County Intermediate Schools
Tecumseh Public Schools (Lenawee)
Traverse Bay Intermediate School District
Trenton Public Schools
Tri-County Center, Incorporated
Tuscola Intermediate School District
University of Michigan
Utica Community Schools
Warren Consolidated Schools
Wayne County Intermediate School District
Wayne State University Rehabilitation Institute
Wayne-Westland Community Schools
Wexford-Missaukee Intermediate School District
Wyoming Physical Handicapped Preschool Program
Washtenaw Intermediate School District
Waterford Public Schools

Oakland-Anderson Junior High School

Minnesota

Minnesota School for the Deaf

Faribault State Hospital

The W. Roby Allen School

Anoka-Hennepin Intermediate School District #11

Austin Public Schools

Crow River Pupil Study Service

Joint Independent School District #287

Cooperative School-Rehabilitation Center

Duluth Public Schools

Lutheran High School

Minneapolis Public Schools

Rochester Public Schools

St. Anthony of Padua School

St. Louis Park Public Schools

St. Paul Program for the Hearing Impaired

East Central Minnesota Special Education Program

Mississippi

Mississippi School for the Deaf

Biloxi Public Schools

Choctaw County Schools

Clarksdale Speech and Hearing Clinic

Columbus Public Schools

University of Mississippi Department of Communicative Disorders

Harrison County Training Center

Jackson County Exceptional School

Jackson Public Schools

Lafayette County Program for the Hearing Impaired

Long Beach Municipal School District

Lowndes County Schools

Magnolia Speech School for the Deaf

McComb Public Schools

Meridian Public Schools

Mississippi State College—Speech Department

School for Children/Language Disorders

South Haven Mennonite School

Tupelo Regional Rehabilitation Center

University of Mississippi Speech and Hearing Clinic

Walthall County Public Schools

Ellisville State School

Missouri

Missouri School for the Deaf

Central Institute for the Deaf

Woodhaven Learning Center

St. Joseph Institute for the Deaf

Child's Mercy Hospital

Columbia Public Schools

Columbia Speech and Hearing Clinic

Gallaudet School for the Deaf

Kansas City School District

Greater Kansas City Hearing and Speech Center

Neosho Public Schools

Nevada R-5 School District

North Kansas City School District

Oakwood Manor Elementary School

St. Joseph School District

Springfield Speech and Hearing Center

Southeast Missouri State College Speech and Hearing Center

St. Louis County Special District

School District R-12—Delaware School

Montana

Montana School for the Deaf

Billings Public Schools

Helena Public Schools

Montana Center for the Handicapped

Missoula Public Schools

Nebraska

Nebraska School for the Deaf

Central Nebraska Speech and Hearing Center

Lincoln Public Schools

Omaha Hearing School

Omaha Public Schools

University of Nebraska Speech and Hearing Center

Nevada

Clark County Day Classes for the Deaf

Mayfair Center—Hard of Hearing Program

Washoe County Schools

New Hampshire

Crotchet Mountain Rehabilitation Center

Amoskeag Center for Educational Services

Concord Union School District

Wall Class for the Hearing Impaired

Portsmouth Rehabilitation Center, Incorporated

Somersworth High School Hearing Impaired Program

Special Education Consortium— Hearing Impaired Program

Supervisory Union #56

New Jersey

Marie Katzenbach School for the Deaf

American Institute for Mental Studies

The Archway School

Avon School

Bancroft School

Bergan County Program for the Deaf

Bloomfield Public Schools

Bordentown City Schools

Bruce Street School

Public Schools of Jersey City

Burlington County Memorial Hospital

Chatham Borough School

Clifton Public Schools

The Deron School for Hearing Handicapped

East Brunswick Public Schools

Elizabeth Public Schools

Kearny Public Schools

Gate House Nursery School

Hard of Hearing Center

Gloucester County Public Schools

Kossuth Street School

Helmbold Educational Center

Hunterdon Medical Center

Kean College of New Jersey

Lake Drive School

Livingston Township Board of Education

Madison Township Schools

The Midland School

Millburn School for Hearing Handicapped

A. Harry Moore Laboratory School

Morris County Board of Education

Morristown Hospital Speech and Hearing Center

Myrtle Avenue School

Neptune Township Public Schools

New Brunswick Board of Education

North Hudson Jointure Commission

North Jersey Training Schools

Oak Crest School

Parsippany Public School

Passaic County Technical and Vocational High School

Patterson Board of Education

Perth Amboy Schools

Piscataway Township Schools

Summit Speech School

Toms River School

Trenton Public Schools

Vineland Public Schools— Cumberland County

West Burlington Regional Schools

Westwood Regional Schools

Ulysses S. Wiggins School

Woodbridge Public Schools

New Mexico

New Mexico School for the Deaf

Albuquerque Public Schools— North Area

Eastern New Mexico University Speech and Hearing Center

Albuquerque Preschool—Hearing Handicapped Program

New York

New York State School for the Deaf, Rome

New York State School for the Deaf, White Plains

St. Mary's School for the Deaf

Rochester School for the Deaf

New York Institute for the Education of the Blind

Lexington School for the Deaf

Albany County BOCES

Albany Medical Center

Center for the Multiple Handicapped Children

Binghampton City School District

Children's Hospital

Orange County BOCES

BOCES Broome County

BOCES Dutchess County

Erie County BOCES

BOCES Nassau County

Monroe County BOCES

Rensselaer-Columbia BOCES

BOCES Rockland County

Suffolk BOCES

Putman Westchester County BOCES

Buffalo Public Schools

Bureau for the Hearing Handicapped—Public School #158

School for Language and Hard of Hearing Children

Children's Hospital and Rehabilitation Center

Cleary School for the Deaf—Ronkonkoma

Cuyahoga County Board—Mental Retardation Program

Home Program, Rochester School for the Deaf

Greater Amsterdam School District

Hamilton School #31

Hebrew Institute for the Deaf

Islip Public Schools

Public School #47

Leicester Educational Center

Meadowbrook Hospital

Mill Neck Manor School for the Deaf

Saratoga-Warren County BOCES

Public School #40

New York League for the Hard of Hearing

Queens College Speech and Hearing Center

Rome State School

Rockland County Center for the Physically Handicapped

Rubella Evaluation Project

St. Francis de Salle School for the Deaf

St. Joseph's School for the Deaf

Schenectady Special Educational District

Special Education, Rochester

Suffolk Developmental Center

Syracuse City School District

Union-Endicott School District

United Cerebral Palsy Center

Upstate Medical Center

Westchester BOCES #11

BOCES—Warren County

North Carolina

North Carolina School for the Deaf

Central North Carolina School for the Deaf

Eastern North Carolina School for the Deaf

Charlotte Speech and Hearing Center

Cumberland County Schools

Duke Speech and Hearing Clinic

Durham City Schools

Gaston County Classes for the Hearing Impaired

Goldsboro City Schools

Nash County Schools

New Hanover County Schools

Preschool Satellite Program at Central North Carolina School for the Deaf

Training Center for the Hearing Impaired Children

Wake County Preschool for the Hearing Impaired

Winston-Salem/Forsyth County Schools

North Dakota

North Dakota School for the Deaf

North Dakota School for the Blind

The Crippled Children's School

Ward County Special Education Program

Opportunity School

University of North Dakota Department of Speech Pathology

Ohio

Ohio School for the Deaf

St. Rita's School for the Deaf

Akron Public Schools

Alexander Graham Bell School—Cleveland

Alexander Graham Bell School—Columbus

Beachwood Board of Education

Canton City Public Schools

Cincinnati Public Schools

Cincinnati Speech and Hearing Center

Clark County Speech and Hearing Center

Cleveland Heights School

Cleveland Hearing and Speech Center

Cuyahoga County Board of Mental Retardation

Edgewood School District

Fulton County Special Education Services Center

Franklin County Program for the Mentally Retarded

Findlay Program for the Hearing Impaired

Kent Public Schools

Interdistrict School for the Hearing Impaired

Litchfield Rehabilitation Center at Summit

Lorain City Schools

Steubenville City Schools

Mansfield City Schools

Miami Valley Regional Center for the Handicapped

Millridge Center for the Hearing Impaired Children

Dayton Public Schools

Secondary Hearing Impaired Program

Springfield City Schools

Stark County Department of Education

Toledo Hearing and Speech Center

Toledo Public Schools

Trumbull County Schools

Trumbull County Hearing Society

West Heights Class for the Hard of Hearing

William Patrick Day Center

Youngstown Public Schools

Zanesville Classes for the Deaf

Hearing and Speech of Dayton-Clark Counties

Oklahoma

Oklahoma School for the Deaf

Jane Brooks School for the Deaf

Community Speech and Hearing Center

Del City Public Schools

Enid Public Schools

Mid-Del Public School System

Moore Public Schools

Muskogee Public Schools

Oklahoma City Public Schools

Shawnee Public Schools

Tulsa Public Schools

Oklahoma University Medical Center

University of Oklahoma Child Study Center

Oregon

Oregon State School for the Deaf

Tucker-Maxon Oral School for the Deaf

Cods County Intermediate Educational District

Corvalis School District #509

Eugene Hearing and Speech Center

Eugene Regional Facility for the Deaf

Fairview Hospital and Training Center

Good Samaritan Hospital—Medical Center

South Oregon Regional Facility for the Deaf

Linn-Benton Intermediate School District

Malheur County Intermediate Educational District

Pendleton School District

Portland Center for Hearing and Speech

Portland Public Schools

Salem Public Schools

Washington County Intermediate Educational District

Pennsylvania

Pennsylvania School for the Deaf

Western Pennsylvania School for the Deaf

Scranton State School for the Deaf

PA Unit 1—Fayette County

PA Unit 3—Allegheny County

PA Unit 4—Butler County

PA Unit 5—Crawford County

PA Unit 6—Clarion County

PA Unit 7—Westmoreland County

PA Unit 8—Bedford County

PA Unit 9—Cameron County

PA Unit 10—Cambria County

PA Unit 11—Fulton County

PA Unit 12—Adams County

PA Unit 13—Lancaster County

PA Unit 14—Berks County

PA Unit 15—Cumberland County

PA Unit 16—Northumberland County

PA Unit 17—Bradford County

PA Unit 18—Luzerne County

PA Unit 19—Lackawanna County

PA Unit 20—Monroe County

PA Unit 21—Carbon County

PA Unit 22—Bucks County

PA Unit 23—Montgomery County

PA Unit 24—Chester County

PA Unit 25—Delaware County

PA Unit 27—Beaver County

PA Unit 28—Armstrong County

PA Unit 29—Schuylkill County

DePaul Institute

Erie City School District

Eye and Ear Hospital at the University of Pittsburgh

Friends of the Deaf Nursery Center

Geisinger Medical Center

Hearing Conservation Center

W.E. Martin School

Pathfinder Exceptional School

Philadelphia Public Schools

Pittsburgh Hearing and Speech Society

Pittsburgh Public Schools

Archbishop Ryan Memorial Institute for the Deaf

St. Christopher's Hospital

Technical Memorial High School

Upsal Day School

Wyoming Valley Association

Easter Seal—York County

Ebensburg State School and Hospital

Elwyn Institute

Home of Merciful Saviour

Overbrook School for the Blind

Pennhurst State School and Hospital

St. Mary of Providence

Western Pennsylvania School for the Blind

White Haven State School and Hospital

The Woods School

Dr. G.A. Barber Center

Bloomsburg State College

Butler County Easter Seal Society

Child Development Center

Church of the Brethren

Delaware Valley School District

Rhode Island

Rhode Island School for the Deaf

Emma Pendleton Bradley Hospital

Nathanael Green School

Rhode Island Easter Seal Society

Rhode Island Hearing and Speech Center

Windmill Hearing Program

South Carolina

South Carolina School for the Deaf

Aikens County School District

Beauford County Schools

Bennettsville Elementary School

Charleston Speech and Hearing Clinic

Charleston County School District

Spartanburg Speech and Hearing Clinic

Hearing and Speech Center— Columbus

Darlington Area Schools

Estes Elementary School

Fairfield County Schools

Florence County Schools

Greenville County School District

Greenwood District #50

Myrtle Heights Elementary School

Pee Dee Speech and Hearing Center

Richland County School District

Seneca Public Schools

Spartanburg County Schools

Williamsburg County Schools

South Dakota

South Dakota School for the Deaf

South Dakota School for the Deaf, Itinerant Program

Aberdeen Public Schools

Rapid City Public Schools

West River Independent School District #18

Tennessee

Tennessee School for the Deaf

Arlington Hospital and School

Orange Grove School

Carter County Board of Education

Greene Valley Developmental Center

Daniel Arthur Rehabilitation Center

Sunnyside Elementary School

Clover Bottom Hospital and School

Eastern Tennessee State University Preschool for the Deaf

Hamilton County Schools

Chatt-Hamilton County Speech and Hearing Center

Harrison-Chilhowee Baptist Academy

Henderson County School for the Deaf

Johnson City Public Schools

Knoxville City Schools

Knox County Schools

Mama Lere Parent Teaching Home Program

Memphis City Schools

Memphis Oral School

Memphis State University Speech and Hearing Center

Peabody College

University of Tennessee Verbo-Tonal Program

West Tennessee Hearing and Speech Center

Metro-Wilkerson Acoustic Preschool Program

Texas

Texas School for the Deaf

Austin State School

Lufkin State School

Lubbock State School

Abilene Independent School District

North Harris County Cooperative

Amarillo Regional Day School for the Deaf

Anahuac Independent School District

Austin Independent School District

Balcones Special Services Cooperative

Bastrop Special Services Cooperative

Baylor University Speech and Hearing Center

Beaumont Regional Educational Program

Newton Jasper School

Birdville Independent School District

San Antonio Regional Day School for the Deaf

Burleson-Milam Special Services Cooperative

Regional School for the Deaf at Brownsville

Regional Day School for the Deaf at Corpus Christi

Brazoria-Fort Bend Cooperative Educational Program

Nacogdoches Independent School District

Bryan Independent School District

Caldwell County Cooperative

Calhoun County Independent School District

Callier Center for Communication Disorders

Children Development Center

Comal Independent School District

South Texas Speech, Hearing and Language Center

Conroe Independent School District

Dallas Regional Day School for the Deaf

Del Valle Independent School District

Denton State School

Regional Day School for the Deaf at Denton

Odessa Regional Day School for the Deaf

Regional School for the Deaf at Edinburg

El Paso County-wide Day School for the Hearing Impaired

Laredo Regional Day School for the Deaf

Giddings Special Services Cooperative

Gonzales County Cooperative

Grayson County Easter Seal Society

Greenville Public Schools

Henderson Independent School District

Harlandale Independent School District

Hays-Blanco Special Education Cooperative

Hereford Independent School District

Hill County Special Education Cooperative

Houston Independent School District

Houston Speech and Hearing Center

Houston School for the Deaf

Irving Regional Day School for the Deaf

Kerrville Regional Day School for the Deaf

Temple Independent School District

Mainland Cooperative

Longview Independent School District

Lubbock Regional Education Program

Lufkin Independent School District

Marble Falls Special Education District

Marlin Independent School District

Multi-County Special Education Cooperative

Mesquite Regional Day School for the Deaf

Midland Independent School District

Moody State School

New Caney Regional Day School for the Deaf

Northeast Independent School District

East Harris Cooperative

Permian Basin Rehabilitation Center

Golden Triangle Cooperative

Freestone, Limestone, Navarro School

Richardson Regional Day School for the Deaf

Region XV Educational Center at San Angelo

San Antonio Independent School District

Seguin Independent School District

San Marcos Independent School District

Sherman Independent School District

Capland Center for Communication Disorders

Sunshine Cottage School

Fort Worth Regional Day School for the Deaf

Texarkana Regional Day School for the Deaf

Texas Tech University Speech and Hearing Clinic

Texas Christian University

Tri-County Program, Copperas Cove

University of Texas Audiology and Speech Pathology Department

Tyler Independent School District

Uvalde Regional Day School for the Deaf

Victoria Public Schools

Waxahachie Regional Day School for the Deaf

Wichita Falls Regional Day School for the Deaf

Willis Independent School District

Williamson County Cooperative for Special Services

Ysletta Independent School District

Utah

Utah School for the Deaf

Edith Bowen Laboratory School

Davis County School District

Granite School District

Jordan School District

Nebo School District

Vermont

Austine School for the Deaf

Vermont Achievement Center

Austine Educational Unit

Virginia

Virginia School for the Deaf at Hampton

Virginia School for the Deaf at Staunton

Albemarle County Schools

Arlington County Public Schools

Washington County Schools

Bristol Speech and Hearing Center

Charlottesville Public Schools

Chesterfield County Public Schools

Old Dominion University

Cooperative School for the Multi-Handicapped

Portsmouth Diagnostic-Adjustment-Corrective Center

Fairfax County Schools

Hampton City Schools

Harrisonburg Public Schools

Medical College of Virginia

Norfolk City Schools

Prince William County Public Schools

Richmond Public Schools

Roanoke City Schools

Spotsylvania County Schools

Tidewater Rehabilitation Institute

Virginia Beach City Schools

Dilenowisco-Dickenson School

Roanoke Speech and Hearing Center

Washington

Washington State School for the Deaf

Washington State School for the Blind

Washington State Cerebral Palsy Center

Aberdeen School District #5

Bellevue Public Schools

Bellingham School District

Bremerton School District

Columbia Basin Child Hearing Program

Spokane Public Schools

Edmonds School District #15

Highline School District #401

Intermediate School District #167

Issaquah School District #411

Kent Public Schools

Lake Washington Special Education Center

Longview School District #122

Mabton School District #120

Snohumish County School District #25

Moses Lake School District #161

Northshore School District #417

Pullman Public Schools Special Services Program

Rainer School

Renton School District #403

Seattle Public Schools

Seattle Speech and Hearing Clinic Nursery Program

Sequim School District #323

Shoreline School District #412

Tacoma Public Schools

Tri-Cities Special Education Program

University of Washington Child Development Center

Warden School District #146-161

Washington State University

Yakima Public Schools

Tri-County-Lincoln School

West Virginia

West Virginia School for the Deaf and the Blind

Cabell County Schools

Fayette County School System

Kanawha County Public Schools

Kanawha Speech and Hearing Center

Marshall University Speech and Hearing Center

Fayette County Board of Education—Mt. Hope

West Virginia University Preschool Class

Wisconsin

Wisconsin School for the Deaf

St. John's School for the Deaf

South Wisconsin Colony and Training School

Appleton Public Schools

Cesa #4, Hearing Impaired Program

Eau Claire Area Public Schools

Sullivan School

Kenosha Unified School District

La Crosse City School District

Milwaukee Hearing Society

Milwaukee Public Schools

Oshkosh Area Public Schools

Pleasant Hill—Waukesha County

Washington Elementary School

Racine Unified School District

Sheboygan Public Schools

Shorewood Public Schools

Superior Day School for the Deaf

Wausau Day School for the Deaf

Wyoming

Wyoming School for the Deaf

Laramie County School District #1

A Listing of Colleges and Universities with Data on Their Graduates from Teacher Training Programs (1957-1979)

This list of training centers at colleges and universities may serve as a quick reference. For more information about such programs of study, admissions requirements, financial aid, or school calendars, the reader should contact the director of specific programs. In the chart, the reader will find:
- name of college or university, listed by states.
- level of program (UG = undergraduate, G = graduate).
- date of program funding.
- number of trainees completing the program for the twenty-two years, 1957-1979.
- total number of program graduates, as reported by the schools to *American Annals of the Deaf.*

Programs approved by the Conference of Executives of American Schools for the Deaf or by the Council on Education of the Deaf have been noted with an asterisk (*).

Source: American Annals of the Deaf Reference Issues *(formerly Directory of Programs and Services for the Deaf). 1957-1979, 102-124.*

College/University	Number of Trainees Completing Teacher Training Programs by Year							
	57	58	59	60	61	62	63	64
Alabama								
*University of Alabama (UG, G) Founded: 1962	—	—	—	—	—	—	2	4
University of Montevallo (UG) Founded: 1974	—	—	—	—	—	—	—	—
Arizona								
*University of Arizona (G) Founded: 1957	—	—	—	—	3	1	12	12
Arkansas								
*University of Arkansas (UG) Founded: 1953	—	—	—	7	—	5	13	10
California								
*California St. Univ., Fresno (UG, G) Founded: 1969	—	—	—	—	—	—	—	—
*California St. Univ., Los Angeles (G) Founded: 1951	—	—	—	10	7	9	14	13
*California St. Univ., Northridge (G) Founded: 1969	—	—	—	—	—	—	—	—
*San Diego State University (UG, G) Founded: 1970	—	—	—	—	—	—	—	—
*San Francisco State University (G) Founded: 1951	—	—	—	9	7	15	22	22
University of Redlands (UG, G) Founded: 1971	—	—	—	—	—	—	—	—
*University of Southern California (G) Founded: 1942	—	—	—	7	5	6	13	11
Colorado								
Colorado State College Founded: 1959	—	—	—	—	—	—	13	—
University of Denver Founded: 1967	—	—	—	—	—	—	—	—

65	66	67	68	69	70	71	72	73	74	75	76	77	78	79	Total Graduates
5	5	5	3	5	5	6	4	9	19	22	23	25	20	15	**177**
—	—	—	—	—	—	—	—	—	—	1	7	11	15	14	**48**
10	14	12	19	22	25	17	24	16	12	12	13	11	12	11	**258**
9	6	6	7	5	6	3	8	8	11	14	9	6	3	3	**139**
—	—	—	—	—	—	11	10	8	13	14	18	10	7	15	**106**
11	9	10	15	18	23	29	35	22	21	13	18	16	12	7	**312**
—	—	—	—	—	—	—	12	20	28	29	15	30	30	30	**194**
—	—	—	—	—	—	—	14	14	12	15	12	15	22	15	**119**
16	9	7	18	10	11	24	21	16	—	2	12	14	19	17	**271**
—	—	—	—	—	—	—	—	6	—	3	—	—	—	—	**9**
12	11	9	10	8	9	8	10	10	10	10	10	10	10	8	**187**
8	10	17	11	16	21	—	—	—	—	—	—	—	—	—	**96**
—	—	—	7	—	3	—	—	—	—	—	—	—	—	—	**10**

College/University	Number of Trainees Completing Teacher Training Programs by Year							
	57	58	59	60	61	62	63	64
*University of Northern Colorado (G) Founded: 1959	—	—	—	—	—	—	—	—
Connecticut								
Southern Connecticut State College (G) Founded: 1974	—	—	—	—	—	—	—	—
District of Columbia								
*Gallaudet College (G) Founded: 1891	—	—	—	25	37	25	28	35
Florida								
*Flagler College (UG) Founded: 1971	—	—	—	—	—	—	—	—
Florida State University (G) Founded: 1967	—	—	—	—	—	—	—	—
University of Miami (G) Founded: 1970	—	—	—	—	—	—	—	—
*University of North Florida (G) Founded: 1973	—	—	—	—	—	—	—	—
University of South Florida (G) Founded: 1974	—	—	—	—	—	—	—	—
Georgia								
*Emory University (G) Founded: 1960	—	—	—	—	—	3	8	5
Georgia State University (G) Founded: 1968	—	—	—	—	—	—	—	—
Illinois								
DePaul University Founded: 1961	—	—	—	—	—	—	5	4
*Illinois State University (UG, G) Founded: 1950	—	—	—	—	—	—	—	10
*MacMurray College (UG) Founded: 1954	—	—	—	—	—	—	3	1
Northern Illinois University (UG) Founded: 1963	—	—	—	—	—	—	—	—

65	66	67	68	69	70	71	72	73	74	75	76	77	78	79	Total Graduates
—	—	—	—	—	—	37	46	49	53	—	59	34	62	40	**380**
—	—	—	—	—	—	—	—	—	—	1	1	4	6	5	**17**
28	12	25	10	13	22	23	21	23	28	34	34	39	38	39	**539**
—	—	—	—	—	—	—	—	—	—	1	5	9	14	15	**44**
—	—	—	—	6	6	10	11	—	—	—	—	—	—	—	**33**
—	—	—	—	—	—	—	4	4	6	—	10	10	13	3	**50**
—	—	—	—	—	—	—	—	—	—	6	8	10	15	19	**58**
—	—	—	—	—	—	—	—	—	—	2	3	3	6	8	**22**
7	4	2	—	3	1	5	4	1	3	2	3	2	2	2	**57**
—	—	—	—	—	3	—	15	20	—	—	20	15	20	15	**108**
6	11	7	7	12	1	—	—	—	—	—	—	—	—	—	**53**
17	16	10	17	16	34	26	39	69	61	17	49	45	34	31	**491**
5	8	10	9	6	1	3	10	12	10	37	23	18	20	20	**160**
—	—	—	—	—	—	13	—	—	—	—	—	—	8	17	**38**

College/University	Number of Trainees Completing Teacher Training Programs by Year							
	57	58	59	60	61	62	63	64
*Northwestern University (G) Founded: 1950	—	—	—	—	4	7	10	5
*University of Illinois at Urbana (UG, G) Founded: 1948	—	—	—	—	—	—	6	8
Indiana								
*Ball State University (UG, G) Founded: 1946	—	—	—	—	—	—	18	23
Butler University Founded: 1960	—	—	—	—	—	2	—	—
Iowa								
University of Iowa (UG, G) Founded: 1936	—	—	—	4	3	3	2	5
Kansas								
*University of Kansas Medical Ctr. (G) Founded: 1951	—	—	—	1	4	2	11	11
Kentucky								
Eastern Kentucky University (UG, G) Founded: 1973	—	—	—	—	—	—	—	—
Louisiana								
*Louisiana State University/ Southern University (UG, G) Founded: 1971	—	—	—	—	—	—	—	—
Our Lady of Holy Cross College (UG) Founded: 1974	—	—	—	—	—	—	—	—
Maryland								
*Western Maryland College (G) Founded: 1966	—	—	—	—	—	—	—	—
Massachusetts								
Boston College (UG, G) Founded: 1957	—	—	—	—	—	—	—	—
Boston University (UG, G) Founded: 1961	—	—	—	—	—	5	14	16

65	66	67	68	69	70	71	72	73	74	75	76	77	78	79	Total Graduates
7	10	10	15	15	17	22	23	18	20	21	19	—	13	5	**241**
10	4	8	6	10	7	11	8	12	12	11	10	12	—	10	**135**
15	33	22	19	22	3	—	30	43	34	37	39	45	48	54	**485**
—	—	—	—	—	—	—	—	—	—	—	—	—	—	—	**2**
4	7	2	2	4	3	3	6	—	—	—	—	—	—	—	**48**
13	12	12	9	12	15	11	13	14	16	20	22	18	9	12	**237**
—	—	—	—	—	—	—	—	—	—	—	—	—	12	6	**18**
—	—	—	—	—	—	—	—	—	2	5	7	9	9	10	**42**
—	—	—	—	—	—	—	—	—	—	—	—	6	2	2	**10**
—	—	—	—	—	—	10	20	20	28	26	102	80	70	70	**426**
—	—	—	—	—	18	14	21	—	—	—	—	—	—	—	**53**
12	16	12	13	19	27	18	16	14	5	12	12	8	14	18	**251**

College/University	Number of Trainees Completing Teacher Training Programs by Year							
	57	58	59	60	61	62	63	64
*Smith College (G) Founded: 1889	—	—	—	23	18	16	18	29
Michigan								
*Eastern Michigan University (UG, G) Founded: 1927	—	—	—	15	10	—	—	—
Michigan State University (UG, G) Founded: 1955	—	—	—	—	—	—	—	—
University of Michigan (G) Founded: 1960	—	—	—	—	—	—	—	—
Wayne State University (UG, G) Founded: 1932	—	—	—	5	3	1	11	10
Minnesota								
University of Minnesota (G) Founded: 1961	—	—	—	—	—	—	12	6
Mississippi								
University of Southern Mississippi (UG, G) Founded: 1966	—	—	—	—	—	—	—	—
Missouri								
*Fontbonne College (UG) Founded: 1960	—	—	—	—	—	—	8	6
*Washington University (UG, G) Founded: 1914	—	—	—	13	22	15	21	21
Nebraska								
*University of Nebraska at Omaha (UG, G) Founded: 1955	—	—	—	—	—	—	5	13
New Hampshire								
University of New Hampshire Founded: 1955	—	—	—	—	—	—	5	8
New Jersey								
*Trenton State College (UG) Founded: 1957	—	—	—	—	14	1	10	7

65	66	67	68	69	70	71	72	73	74	75	76	77	78	79	Total Graduates
23	20	25	23	20	25	20	30	30	26	26	25	26	24	25	**472**
—	—	16	18	25	21	37	35	46	35	38	40	38	28	29	**431**
—	—	—	—	—	—	—	—	26	18	23	24	20	24	18	**153**
4	5	2	—	—	—	—	—	4	—	—	—	—	—	—	**15**
10	6	6	8	10	10	—	25	40	—	20	—	—	—	—	**165**
7	6	4	7	8	7	6	8	12	12	15	10	11	—	5	**136**
—	—	—	—	—	—	—	—	5	5	1	7	5	8	6	**37**
8	11	11	14	13	8	10	10	14	12	12	12	15	12	12	**188**
17	23	20	15	20	22	23	25	24	16	22	22	15	19	17	**392**
11	—	7	4	6	6	—	7	12	10	15	13	13	10	10	**142**
11	—	—	—	—	—	—	—	—	—	—	—	—	—	—	**24**
5	6	13	10	14	12	13	—	—	24	21	21	13	18	18	**220**

College/University	Number of Trainees Completing Teacher Training Programs by Year							
	57	58	59	60	61	62	63	64
New Mexico								
Eastern New Mexico University Founded: 1962	—	—	—	—	—	—	5	—
New York								
*Canisius College (G) Founded: 1914	—	—	—	14	11	14	12	12
Hunter College of City University of New York (G) Founded: 1952	—	—	—	—	—	—	—	—
*New York University (G) Founded: 1962	—	—	—	—	—	—	10	10
*State University College at Geneseo (G) Founded: 1967	—	—	—	—	—	—	—	—
Syracuse University Founded: 1947	—	—	—	5	4	—	5	5
*Teachers College, Columbia Univ. (G) Founded: 1906	—	—	—	12	14	15	23	30
University of Buffalo Founded: 1914	—	—	—	—	—	—	—	—
North Carolina								
Appalachian State University Founded: 1903	—	—	—	—	—	—	—	—
*Atlantic Christian College (UG) Founded: 1969	—	—	—	—	—	—	—	—
*Lenoir-Rhyne College (UG) Founded: 1894	—	—	—	5	6	8	10	14
University of North Carolina (G) Founded: 1976	—	—	—	—	—	—	—	—
North Dakota								
*Minot State College (UG, G) Founded: 1962	—	—	—	—	—	—	9	4
Ohio								
*Bowling Green State University (UG) Founded: 1973	—	—	—	—	—	—	—	—

65	66	67	68	69	70	71	72	73	74	75	76	77	78	79	Total Graduates
6	7	8	7	7	8	8	—	—	—	—	—	—	—	—	**56**
15	14	17	19	18	19	14	19	20	21	21	16	20	23	20	**339**
—	10	15	8	11	10	14	20	20	25	27	20	30	30	30	**270**
10	11	14	11	11	17	14	—	23	32	25	30	40	40	40	**338**
—	—	—	—	3	5	6	10	13	10	10	6	15	15	20	**113**
5	5	1	—	—	—	—	—	—	—	—	—	—	—	—	**30**
25	28	29	24	28	27	25	26	26	31	30	24	20	15	15	**467**
—	—	—	—	—	—	—	—	—	—	—	—	—	—	—	**—**
—	6	—	—	—	15	—	—	—	—	—	—	—	—	—	**21**
—	—	—	—	—	—	—	3	9	11	18	15	16	19	20	**111**
15	9	13	13	12	—	14	10	—	20	21	21	26	25	22	**264**
—	—	—	—	—	—	—	—	—	—	—	—	—	3	2	**5**
3	7	6	6	6	6	8	6	5	5	—	6	—	8	6	**91**
—	—	—	—	—	—	—	—	—	—	—	—	—	—	31	**31**

College/University	57	58	59	60	61	62	63	64
	Number of Trainees Completing Teacher Training Programs by Year							
Cincinnati Bible College (UG) Founded: 1978	—	—	—	—	—	—	—	—
*Kent State University (UG, G) Founded: 1949	—	—	—	—	—	—	14	19
The Ohio State University (G) Founded: 1972	—	—	—	—	—	—	—	2
*University of Cincinnati (G) Founded: 1962	—	—	—	—	—	—	6	10
Oklahoma								
Oklahoma College of Liberal Arts Founded: 1953	—	—	—	8	7	6	10	14
*The University of Tulsa (UG) Founded: 1966	—	—	—	—	—	—	—	—
*University of Oklahoma Health Science Center (G) Founded: 1947	—	—	—	3	2	4	—	3
University of Sciences & Arts of Oklahoma (UG) Founded: 1945	—	—	—	—	—	—	—	—
Oregon								
*Lewis and Clark College (G) Founded: 1950	—	—	—	—	—	—	—	—
*Oregon College of Education(G) Founded: 1960	—	—	—	—	5	7	11	12
*Pacific University (G) Founded: 1972	—	—	—	—	—	—	—	—
Pennsylvania								
Bloomsburg State College (G) Founded: 1971	—	—	—	—	—	—	—	—
*Pennsylvania State University (UG, G) Founded: 1963	—	—	—	—	—	—	—	8
Temple University (G) Founded: 1973	—	—	—	—	—	—	—	—
*University of Pittsburgh (G) Founded: 1926	—	—	—	—	—	—	13	15

65	66	67	68	69	70	71	72	73	74	75	76	77	78	79	Total Graduates
—	—	—	—	—	—	—	—	—	—	—	—	—	—	—	**0**
18	18	19	26	—	18	30	—	44	47	52	50	—	60	31	**446**
3	4	8	—	—	—	—	—	—	5	6	15	12	8	15	**78**
9	8	8	11	14	16	29	—	14	16	21	22	17	10	5	**216**
11	15	8	14	22	14	—	—	—	—	—	—	—	—	—	**129**
—	—	—	—	—	—	2	4	5	6	7	11	7	7	9	**58**
5	10	11	12	14	15	—	11	9	6	9	7	5	5	5	**136**
—	—	—	—	—	—	—	—	—	—	8	8	8	4	—	**28**
—	—	—	—	—	20	18	18	20	20	21	21	22	22	20	**202**
14	13	18	18	19	21	19	20	28	17	19	15	14	18	17	**305**
—	—	—	—	—	—	—	—	—	—	5	6	6	—	5	**28**
—	—	—	—	—	—	—	—	1	8	14	14	14	18	14	**83**
8	9	11	14	13	10	13	18	20	20	25	25	25	25	25	**269**
—	—	—	—	—	—	—	—	—	—	—	—	—	7	10	**17**
15	11	12	10	14	18	11	18	15	16	16	21	17	22	20	**264**

College/University	Number of Trainees Completing Teacher Training Programs by Year							
	57	58	59	60	61	62	63	64
South Carolina								
*Converse College (UG) Founded: 1949	—	—	—	4	7	9	6	7
South Dakota								
*Augustana College (UG, G) Founded: 1955	—	—	—	4	9	5	7	13
Tennessee								
George Peabody College for Teachers Founded: 1909	—	—	—	—	—	—	—	9
Memphis State University (G) Founded: 1974	—	—	—	—	—	—	—	—
*University of Tennessee (UG, G) Founded: 1938	—	—	—	1	3	3	11	11
Texas								
Lamar University (UG, G) Founded: 1969	—	—	—	—	—	—	—	—
*Southern Methodist University (UG, G) Founded: 1968	—	—	—	—	—	—	—	—
Texas Christian University (UG) Founded: 1967	—	—	—	—	—	—	—	—
Texas Tech University (UG) Founded: 1967	—	—	—	—	—	—	—	—
Texas Woman's University (UG, G) Founded: 1960	—	—	—	—	—	—	—	—
*Trinity University (UG, G) Founded: 1954	—	—	—	—	—	—	—	—
University of Houston Founded: 1963	—	—	—	—	—	—	—	—
*University of Texas at Austin (UG, G) Founded: 1920	—	—	—	—	—	—	6	10
Utah								
*University of Utah, Graduate School of Education (G) Founded: 1962	—	—	—	—	—	—	5	6

65	66	67	68	69	70	71	72	73	74	75	76	77	78	79	Total Graduates
6	8	8	7	7	8	7	8	9	8	—	4	1	10	6	**130**
16	5	11	14	14	14	—	14	20	23	20	25	25	14	15	**268**
8	—	5	4	2	—	—	—	—	—	—	—	—	—	—	**28**
—	—	—	—	—	—	—	—	—	—	—	—	—	—	—	**0**
9	8	10	10	16	18	18	25	40	55	70	45	62	51	56	**522**
—	—	—	—	—	—	—	—	—	—	12	15	12	10	12	**61**
—	—	—	—	—	7	6	9	15	28	19	26	13	18	13	**154**
—	—	—	—	—	—	—	4	2	11	16	12	14	14	12	**85**
—	—	—	—	—	—	—	—	—	18	20	20	18	15	8	**99**
—	—	—	—	—	—	—	—	—	—	12	30	26	23	14	**105**
—	—	6	13	5	14	14	18	20	15	19	20	16	22	20	**202**
—	—	—	—	—	—	—	—	11	10	12	—	—	—	—	**33**
12	11	8	13	14	19	20	23	27	24	24	23	23	22	16	**295**
6	7	7	7	6	6	10	9	12	9	7	9	9	8	9	**132**

College/University	Number of Trainees Completing Teacher Training Programs by Year							
	57	58	59	60	61	62	63	64
Virginia								
*University of Virginia (G) Founded: 1967	—	—	—	—	—	—	—	—
Washington								
*University of Washington (G) Founded: 1968	—	—	—	6	5	5	9	8
Wisconsin								
*University of Wisconsin at Milwaukee (UG, G) Founded: 1913	—	—	—	1	7	6	8	7

65	66	67	68	69	70	71	72	73	74	75	76	77	78	79	Total Graduates
—	—	—	2	6	5	—	8	10	5	9	5	12	8	3	**73**
—	9	5	13	15	3	9	12	14	14	15	15	15	13	15	**190**
9	10	9	6	11	13	13	24	23	13	17	10	12	15	26	**240**

One of the most rewarding areas in specialized education is that of teaching the deaf. Although this area is in the general field of education, it is closely allied with the fields of medicine, psychology, speech, language disorders, electronics, rehabilitation, audiology, public health, and social work. Because this area of teaching is so specialized, additional training is necessary.

The need for teachers in this area of special education is acute. A scarcity of qualified persons exists throughout the United States and Canada. Positions are available in public and private residential schools, day schools, and in day classes.

Trained teachers of the deaf are also needed in many speech and hearing clinics located in colleges and universities, schools for the deaf, private centers, hospitals, and in medical schools.

Scholarships are available for teacher trainees in a majority of the training centers.

Evaluation, Approval, and Certification

Directors of training centers making application for evaluation and approval of a teacher education program should write to: Ralph L. Hoag, Ed.D., Chairman, Teacher Training and Certification Committee, Conference of Executives of American Schools for the Deaf, Arizona State School for the Deaf and Blind, 1200 W. Speedway, P.O. Box 5545, Tucson, Arizona 85703.

Teachers of the deaf making application for certification should write: Roy M. Stelle, M.S., Secretary, Teacher Training and Certification Committee, Conference of Executives of American Schools for the Deaf, Arizona State School for the Deaf and Blind, 1200 W. Speedway, P.O. Box 5545, Tucson, Arizona 85703.

Reprinted with permission of American Annals of the Deaf, *1970,* 115, *3.*

About the Authors

Carl J. Jensema has been profoundly deaf since the age of nine. He obtained a Bachelor's degree from Wisconsin State University, a Master's degree from Claremont Graduate School, and a Doctorate in psychometrics from the University of Washington. In 1972 he was a National Science Foundation post-doctoral fellow at the University of California at Berkeley and was also a visiting scholar at Stanford University. After working briefly at the University of Illinois, he accepted an appointment at Gallaudet College, where he spent six years teaching and conducting research. Since 1979 he has been Director of Research at the National Captioning Institute.

Edward E. Corbett, Jr., was born deaf to deaf parents in Louisiana. He received a Bachelor's degree in psychology from Gallaudet College, a Master's in educational administration and supervision from California State University at Northridge, and a Doctorate in special education administration from Gallaudet College. From 1976 to January, 1980, Dr. Corbett served as Assistant Superintendent at the Maryland School for the Deaf, Frederick and Columbia campuses. Prior to coming to the Maryland School, he was responsible for the development of a community education concept involving hearing-impaired people throughout the state of Delaware. He also implemented a mainstreaming concept utilizing interpreter/tutors to help facilitate the communication process for hearing-impaired students attending elementary and secondary programs. Dr. Corbett started his professional career as a teacher at the Louisiana State School for the Deaf where he taught graphic arts and academic subjects to junior high school students. Currently, he is the Director of the National Academy of Gallaudet College in Washington, D.C.

This book was typeset in Univers by Harlowe Typography, Inc., of Brentwood, Maryland. It was printed and bound by Bookcrafters, Inc., of Chelsea, Michigan. The text and cover were designed by Donna Simons.